12/23/75

Young Children Thinking

By the same author

The Teacher of Young Children
The *Young Children Learning* Series
Reaching Out
Exploration and Language
Discovering the Physical World
Senses and Sensitivity

Young Children Thinking

Alice Yardley

Principal Lecturer in Education,
Nottingham College of Education

Citation Press New York 1973

Published by Evans Brothers Limited
Montague House, Russell Square, London, WC1B 5BX

Citation Press, Library and Trade Division, Scholastic Magazines, Inc.
50 West 44th St., New York, New York 10036

Library of Congress Catalog Card Number: 72-96705

Set in 10 on 12 point Baskerville
and printed in Great Britain by T. and A. Constable Ltd.,
Hopetoun Street, Edinburgh.

Standard Book Number 590-07331-1   PRA 3424

Contents

Introduction

There is much in present-day teaching practice to indicate important advances in the education of young children. Learning is usually based on personal experience. Due recognition is given to the significance of individual differences. Understanding is seen as a growth process which cannot be hastened, and children are encouraged to learn fully at each stage in development without being urged on to the next. Motivation is recognised as the key to involvement of the whole person, and learning through personal interest is considered important. At the same time, teachers believe that learning is enhanced by a well-organised environment, and by skilful planning of each activity and situation to ensure progression and profitable experience. Education today is a radically different procedure from practice in the early part of the century, and the role of the teacher has undergone a metamorphosis which would make it scarcely recognisable to our predecessors.

We could attribute this advancement to improved knowledge of children and of the learning process. In many respects we have made good use of twentieth-century discoveries about the child. Excellent as these advances are, however, there are certain important findings which remain virtually disregarded. Even the most observant of adults is still comparatively unaware of the young child's powers of thinking. Too often we

7

try to tell children what to think; we rarely use to the full their powers of thought, and much of the child's cognitive development never reaches its full potential because it remains unchallenged.

We have been clearly shown, by Piaget and others, that children can and do think at every stage in development. The young child has neither the words nor the modes of verbal communication with which to crystallise and convey the patterns of thought which take shape in his infant mind. It is easy for the busy adult to misinterpret, or overlook, such evidence of thought as is possible to young children. We tend to forget that they can and do think about most of the things which happen to them. We often substitute memorising for understanding because we feel that is all they are capable of. We forget to take their thoughts into account and consequently the tasks we set them lack intellectual grip. Although many of us know the facts of intellectual growth, there is a vast difference between knowledge and understanding, between acknowledging and discussing theory and giving practical expression to it in classroom practice.

A future trend in the education of young children lies in this direction, and the aim of this book is to provide simple practical suggestions for adding intellectual dimensions to the child's curriculum. It is not through the addition of subjects and exercises that this can be achieved. It is more a matter of examining the quality of what already exists, of reorientating the events of the day and finding in them a means of stimulating greater activity of the mind on the part of the child.

There is much in present-day practice which is good. What education should aim for is excellence, and where we find it we find reality in learning; education which is full of meaning and which will in truth effect radical changes in behaviour on the part of the individual.

Much that we are taught we forget, but where changes in thought and in the person himself have been affected, this is

8

what constitutes real learning. Learning in depth can only be achieved when what is trivial, superficial and misdirected is pruned away and when each opportunity for experience is fully explored and utilised. We are not called upon to make dramatic changes, but to revitalise existing practice and ensure for each child the fullest possible opportunity for intellectual growth.

Alice Yardley

1

Some facts about mental development

This book is concerned with the practical application of principles rather than with the theory from which these principles are derived. In this chapter, some important facts about mental development are explained in the hope that they may serve as a guide to classroom practice. For those teachers who wish to study the findings of research and the theory which supports these facts, I have provided a select list of books, pamphlets and other documents in the Appendix. We shall here concern ourselves with only the essential core of these works.

The significance of the early years of life cannot be over-estimated. Learning takes place more rapidly between birth and four years than during any other comparable period of time. Growth rate, both physically and mentally, starts fast, reaches mid-point between four and five and then begins to slow down. Between birth and four, 50% of general intelligence develops, 30% between four and eight, and 20% between eight and seventeen. The child's speech and vocabulary, which later provide the foundation of his academic skills, follow a similar pattern of growth and 33% of the child's academic skills are attained before he is six, 42% between the ages of six and thirteen, and 25% between the ages of thirteen and eighteen.

The human baby has few accomplishments at birth. He can

cry, move and suck. His organs function. His sense organs are active. He can react emotionally. On this foundation all later learning depends and everything else the child accomplishes has to be learned. This means that the environment in which learning takes place has a profound effect. While it can never fully compensate for hereditary deficiencies, it can provide opportunity for maximum growth.

Because the human baby has much to learn, he becomes an active agent in his own learning, he helps to shape his own growth. There are genetically-based differences in human temperament, and the part played by each child in his own development is unique from birth.

The sequence of events in development is predetermined, but the rate at which various abilities emerge can be affected by external stimulation. In other words, opportunities in the environment have a considerable influence over the speed at which development takes place and lack of opportunity can inhibit physical and mental activity. The child who has little chance of taking an active interest in the world, can lose the habit of being interested.

Mental operations take place as a result of internalised experiences. The sensory-motor activities of the young child offer him a means of obtaining information about the physical world. He learns to manipulate his materials in purposeful ways and thought activities arise from these concrete operations. He can assimilate and retain what he has done. When confronted by a fresh situation, he can recall and use previous experience to solve an immediate problem, and later, to anticipate a possible problem and provide a solution in advance.

Each of the child's physical experiences is embodied in how he feels emotionally at the time of the experience. What he recalls at a later stage is coloured by his emotions. The child's thinking is very closely interwoven with his sensory and emotional reactions. Thinking and feeling are fused, and reasoning is often based on emotion rather than on fact.

Healthy vigorous mental development depends to a great extent on a good emotional climate, and the hungry or unhappy child is virtually incapable of profitable mental activity.

A key factor in any learning situation is motivation. Mental activity, as any other form of activity, needs challenge, and it is a responsibility of parents and teachers to ensure challenge in the learning situation. While the challenge should be demanding enough to stir the child into using all his resources, it should contain the possibility of achievement. A degree of frustration, disappointment and difficulty is good, too great a challenge defeats its own purpose. Effort and pleasure are the ingredients of constructive thinking, and a mental task should bring the reward of satisfactory accomplishment.

All the concepts we deal with as adults have their origin in the earliest experiences. The quality of embryonic stages of thinking determines the quality of ideas and thought in adult life. Abstract ideas which are the raw material of thought must have sound conceptual foundations if thought activity is to be of a high level. Early thought activity arises from concrete situations, and the quality of environmental opportunity will determine the quality of adult ideas. What we feel, see and hear physically is the material from which thought emerges, and the adult is responsible for the kinds of sense experiences which are available to the child during his formative years.

Finally, there is a close connection between words and thought, and at all stages language development is crucial to thought activity. The two are not identical, but they are interdependent, and the context within which the child acquires language has a permanent influence over the way he learns to think.

While the connection between language and mental activity is not given separate treatment in this book, in each situation the contribution of speech and language activity will be given its rightful importance. In *Exploration and Language*, one of the

13

books in the 'Young Children Learning' series, the development of language and its role in learning is more closely examined.

There are many other factors affecting mental growth, but those we consider here will serve as a framework of reference around which a teacher can plan much of her work.

2

Before going to school

The implications of these facts for pre-school development are enormous. The foundation for the child's thought processes has already been laid before he enters school and, although this book is mainly concerned with the vitality of education during the early years of obligatory schooling, some reference to pre-school experience cannot be omitted. The major responsibility in the early years, of course, rests with the parents, but teachers can only carry the child on in his development if they are thoroughly familiar with events in the pre-school stages.

What view do parents take of their child's early thinking? One parent of a two-year-old said to me recently, 'Watching him grow up is a fascinating experience. I shall never forget the first time he expressed a thought that I hadn't put into his mind.'

This father was delighted to discover that so young a child had an independent opinion. He now encourages his son to voice his views. He asks his opinion on relevant matters, and having listened to what his little boy has to say, tries to act on it.

'I try to involve my children in family affairs as soon as they can understand,' another parent explained. 'Even Lisa (two years) likes to feel we include her when we're making important plans. We've just moved into a new house and Lisa's chosen the paper for her bedroom from the patterns in the book.'

Kathie was only a toddler when her mother began to treat her as a person who was capable of making a decision. 'We're going to Aunty Beryl's for tea,' she explained. 'See. I'll put your dresses on the bed and you can tell me which one you would like to wear today.'

When observing very young babies, I am always amazed at the highly intelligent way in which they deal with early learning. Meeting some of these babies a few years later, it would seem that intelligent behaviour is deteriorating and by the time they are in the Secondary School the question arises, 'What has happened?' Promising intelligence now seems virtually extinct.

The pre-speech child has a distinct advantage in that because he has no words, he is protected from being told what to learn and how to learn it, and how to solve his problems.

Loving adults are filled with compassion for the helpless child and, unable to bear his painful groping, they try to make the problem easy to solve by showing him the best way to deal with it. In so doing, they rob him of essential stimulation, reduce the amount of effort he puts into the task and eventually his unused resources begin to dwindle.

In the early days of life, the child's immediate environment presents a very high level of challenge. The simple problems of attracting adult attention, of grasping the tempting object, of improving his powers of locomotion in order to get from here to there, all require his full attention and he accomplishes these feats with little assistance. We need to maintain this high level of challenge and the best means of doing so is to introduce the child to problems of increasing difficulty and then to ensure maximum effort on his part by keeping adult assistance to a bare minimum. He learns speech all too quickly, and while speech is an essential part of thought equipment, it also provides the means of adult instruction, and the more the child is told how to do things, the less he thinks for himself.

Problems for the very young child arise mainly at a physical level through motor involvement with the environment. Some of the most educative situations occur as often through every-day living as through expensive equipment such as construc-tional toys.

From the age of eighteen months, Pamela found dressing and undressing a most absorbing occupation. For several weeks she pulled off her socks and shoes as often as her mother put them on. Then came the day when she tried to put on her own sock. As often as not the heel appeared on top of her foot, and when it did she pulled it and looked puzzled. After struggling for two weeks, she could fit the sock to her foot as she put it on. This she did a number of times with intense pleasure. Pamela had an understanding mother who allowed her to grope for her own solution, even though it held up the dressing process interminably some mornings.

From the moment of birth the young child is remarkably responsive to his environment. He reacts at every point to what is happening round him. He doesn't just receive experience, he becomes totally involved in it, and his active participation modifies both the environment and the effect it has on him. In other words, the child himself plays an essential role in his own growth and is to a considerable extent the architect of his own personality.

What the child brings to each situation has much to do with the quality of experience gained in it. He may have certain capabilities built into his cells. This is not the same thing as having intelligence. The child's mind and intellectual qualities grow, and it is through a series of interactions with the environ-ment that the ultimate stature of the child's mind is determined. It is a unified whole which is constantly growing and being re-structured as a result of his active participation in experience.

As in other aspects of development, there is a sequence of stages through which the mind develops towards maturity and these stages cannot be altered. As each stage unfolds, the quality of experience leaves its indelible effect. Each stage grows out of the stage which precedes it and provides the foundation for the next stage. The ultimate structure of the mind retains all previous structures, and flaws or insecure foundations remain part of its stature for the rest of the child's life.

The baby naturally reaches out to learn, but subsequent events can encourage, or discourage, this natural habit. In the second year of life, for instance, the concept of permanence is established. Until the child understands, without any shadow of doubt, that objects hold their characteristic structure and remain in existence whether he can see and feel them or not, he can develop no further in thought. The ability to think involves the recall of mental images and only the permanence of objects and matter makes these images useful in thought. The child who is encouraged to be mobile, who is given ample opportunity to handle and manipulate materials and objects in a well-stocked environment is given a helpful start. But how does a child learn about the nature and characteristics of what his environment holds if he is strapped for long waking hours in a high chair, isolated in a play-pen, or restricted to a small play area in a high flat? How far is he free to react and develop his mind if activity is frowned upon? Mothers who pride themselves on having quiet, passive babies which grow into toddlers who cause no commotion and rarely get dirty are denying their children the opportunity to become intelligent.

The child needs intellectual challenge from his earliest days. We don't wait in hope for his mind to grow and then provide it with experiences of interest, we stimulate and encourage it with what quickens the intellect. At the same time, the emotional climate in which the child is reared is equally important. The baby's experiences are global and each experience is embodied in his emotional state at the moment he experiences it. How he feels in a physical and emotional sense impregnates each

18

experience, and recall of the images left by the experience bring with them all that was happening to his person.

The parent, then, is responsible for the emotional and intellectual environment in which growth of the mind takes place. The citizen of the future is shaped during these early days. By the time the child enters school, the plans have already been designed and the foundations laid. One third of his ultimate intellectual skills will have been mastered by the time he is six and the growth of his brain is largely completed by the age of seven. Improving the child's chances at 15 by offering him an extra year of education, or providing special tuition for the slower or handicapped child from the age of seven, may bring little benefit. The time to provide him with help is before he is six, and preferably during the first four years of life. On these grounds alone could the case for pre-school education be pressed home. So far, the provision of pre-school education has depended on social and economic factors and little attention has been paid to acknowledged fact of intellectual growth.

This is not to say that state-organised education in the pre-school years is necessarily the only, or even the best solution. In the emotionally warm and orderly way of life of a stable home the child can find much of what he needs for full vigorous growth, and the ultimate quality of society depends on well-educated parents; that is on parents who understand as well as love. Education for parenthood at the moment is mainly a matter of handing on from generation to generation the way of life which characterises a family, and state schools rarely construct a curriculum with parenthood in mind. The Newsom Report pointed the way towards 'courses built round broad themes of home-making' and 'partnership in marriage', and recommended, for both boys and girls, 'a range of rewarding studies . . . basically related to domestic crafts and interests, but reaching out both into the humanities and into science' (*See pp 388-401*).

Schemes of this kind are being tried in a few schools with

rewarding results, and as school life becomes longer it is hoped that such realistic courses for children on the brink of adult life will become widespread in all types of schools. It isn't just the Newsom children who become parents; some of our most intelligent parents remain the least well educated as far as being home- and marriage-makers is concerned.

3

Involvement in social education

One of the major advantages to the child on entering school is the social situation in which it involves him. Here he can meet many children of a similar age along with significant adults outside his family circle and be introduced through this micro-society to the wider world of the cultural group in which his home plays a part. He is at this stage prepared to think about a number of important social issues. He is not merely emotionally involved. His mental abilities are equally activated by the situation, and with the aid of the adult the child's rudimentary thinking can be vastly improved.

We have a good example in Vietnam at the moment of what happens when the child is deprived of social education. There are about a quarter of a million young children at present in Vietnamese orphanages. A single untrained helper is responsible for twenty children. There is little time and each child is caged in an iron cot and left alone. At feeding time a bottle is propped on a cushion and there are no opportunities for play. One little three-year-old looks and behaves like a six-month-old baby and shows little sign of mental activity, but she did not die within the first year in the orphanage as 90% of her companions did.

A few months ago, a play-group was formed in her orphanage by the Gordon Barclay Vietnam Fund and the transformation has been miraculous. She is learning to walk and to laugh, and her mental age grows daily. She will soon be normal.

What was so vital to her in the experience a play-group provided? What made the difference between life and death?

The importance to the child of social activity is apparent from the moment of birth when child and mother meet. Loving adults fully acknowledge the emotional needs of the child as a social being, but is this all there is to it? Mark is nearly four. He has an excellent home and fully adequate love and attention from his parents, yet a vital factor is lacking, and his mother brings him to the play-group because, as she puts it, 'He needs the stimulation of other children and I don't want him to get too dependent on me'. Mark has an active mind and he readily responds to the challenge of other minds. Contact with the wider world brings him more fully alive, because it extends him mentally as well as in other ways.

When the child of five enters school he is intellectually aware of his need for contact with other people, and the social situation contains much to challenge mental activity. If he is emotionally prepared to join a group, he is anxious to be accepted as a member of it. At the same time he fears losing his newly-found self-identity, and many children are torn between wanting to belong and fearing to lose their recognition as an individual. 'How will the teacher know me,' Sandra complained, 'when all these others look the same?'

This situation offers an excellent opportunity for the teacher to help the child to understand something of individual differences. 'Let's go over to the mirror,' said one reception class teacher with five newly admitted children. 'Look at yourself. Do you know which is you? How do you know? Who has curly hair?' etc., etc..

This investigation continued for several minutes. The children became absorbed. The teacher then produced labels on which she had written each child's name. 'This is Wendy Pratt.' She showed the children the name and Wendy claimed her label. 'This is Wendy. She looks like Wendy and nobody else. When I see Wendy and say, "Wendy Pratt", there is only one of her wherever we are.'

The children then turned their attention to names and went round the room asking other children what their names were. 'I'm Pratt,' Wendy explained to another child, 'because I belong to Mum and Dad and they're called Mr and Mrs Pratt.' The same teacher later used the names labels as the basis of her introduction to reading.

Belonging obliges the child to accept a social role prescribed by the group, and as the child grows older he can find answers to such questions as 'Why do you like to play with so and so?' and by so doing become aware of what is required of him too. Social insight is by no means exclusively a characteristic of intelligent children and, in the field of social awareness, the otherwise duller child often finds the chance to excel. The school itself is a social unit with a characteristic structure and the function of its various members is a source of great interest to the child. The Head Teacher, the Caretaker, the School Secretary, have definite functions and the child can be introduced to the structure of a society by observation of their various roles.

A major social task at this stage is learning to share an activity. Early experiments are usually a matter of trial and error, often accompanied by squabbling and perhaps a few tears. Eventually a state of harmony emerges and two children discover the additional benefits to be obtained from a partnership. They are then in a position to consider the situation. Where young children are concerned, thinking grows out of action. At a later stage, thinking gives rise to action, as well as following action.

James and Doug both wanted the large plastic bus. First they struggled for sole possession. Eventually James announced, 'You can get on. I'll push you and then you can push me.' The fun lasted for several minutes. During a quieter moment later on in the day, their teacher asked, 'Did you enjoy your game with the bus? Is it more fun with two people?' James stared at the bus for a moment and then replied, 'It's more fun when somebody pushes me, but I don't mind pushing Doug if he pushes me'. His mind was already dealing with the idea of give and take in a partnership and verbalising helped him to crystallise the idea.

At this stage in development, many children are puzzled by relationships between members of their own family. A child may hear Mother referred to as sister, auntie, daughter, wife. At first this may be amusing, but later it becomes confusing. Rebecca, an intelligent little girl of five, had three brothers. She recounted their names when asked by her teacher, 'Who else have you in your family?' 'There's John and Phillip and Richard,' she said and in a moment added, 'They're brothers.' 'If they are brothers,' her teacher asked, 'What are you?' After a slight hesitation Rebecca replied, 'I'm a girl brother'.

A family of dolls can be helpful in this kind of situation. Grandmother, Grandfather, Mother and Father, big brother and sister and toddler brother and sister, can be used as a concrete aid when talking out with the child the relation of one to another. Once the child has grasped the idea within his own family, he can relate it to other family groups. The concept of the family group as belonging to each of the other children in the class fascinates some children, and the idea that the teacher is similarly a member of a family may not be grasped for some time.

Friendship between young children is an extremely fluid social situation. Early companionship is often determined by geographical conditions and during the first days in school a child may tend to associate with 'the boy next door' simply because he is more familiar than the other children. Group play enables him to learn about other children, and very soon children begin to select playmates according to their pre- ferences and because they find them challenging and therefore interesting as companions. At this stage many children are ready to discuss the playmate experience and what is meant by friendship.

Five-year-old children described a friend as 'Somebody to play with'. 'A boy or a girl.' 'So's I don't feel lonely.' 'Another boy I like.' 'We do the same things.' 'I lend her my dolly's iron and then she gives me her feeding bottle.' Friendship is a difficult concept, but clearly the embryonic idea had already been formed.

Friendship with other children leads to visiting the homes of others. Many children expect the home of a friend to be virtually identical with their own. Terry returned home from his first party. 'What do you think, Mum,' he puzzled, 'They don't go to bed in Tony's house. There aren't any stairs.' On the evidence as he understood it, Terry had drawn certain conclusions. He needed the help of the adult to expand his basic concept of the home. Terry became intensely interested in homes and houses. His mother and teacher were in contact, and Terry was helped by his teacher to expand his ideas to include the homes of many different kinds in the United Kingdom. It was an exciting event to discover that people he met in the street came from many different kinds of backgrounds.

This growing awareness of the lives of others is often evident to visitors to a classroom. The six- and seven-year-olds usually want to identify the unfamiliar person. 'What is your name?' is a means of labelling, of reducing a situation to something comprehensible and of removing some of the fear of the unknown. 'Where do you come from?' 'What do you do?' 'Are you Miss So-and-so's mother?'

Here again the teacher is offered an excellent starting point for the child's study of what makes a society. She is a means of introducing him to fundamental social units outside his home. Through his contact with different members of society she can help him to understand its structure and the way in which it is held together by the social laws of service and co-operation, and even the elementary principles of democratic government. 'Why are you a teacher?' opens up all kinds of possibilities. The fact that the situation has occasioned the question is an index, not only of the child's interest, but of his dawning comprehension. Visitors to the school and representatives of outside agencies are a tremendous mental challenge at this stage, and the child can benefit enormously from what sometimes appears, from the teacher's point of view, to be an interruption.

The concepts of social structure are complex, but put in simple form to the child, they are within his powers of comprehension. In the school situation we have a simply structured community, and by becoming aware of the community of which he is an important part, the child is able to formulate some basic ideas about group structure. By the time he leaves the Infant School he has sufficient experience of this intimate community and of agencies outside it to understand the position the school group holds in the wider pattern. These ideas provide a foundation on which the general cultural ideas of his own society will develop.

Perhaps the greatest challenge to the child in his first years in school, for instance, is the whole complicated business of group organisation. Even the youngest children realise that assembling a large number of children and expecting them to work and play together creates problems which don't exist when there are only two or three. Conflict over the use of tools and materials is often the starting point and when some of the heat has gone out of the situation, the child's feelings give rise to thinking. 'What can we do about it?' can turn the conflict into a matter of interest.

In the next chapter we will consider the organisation of the classroom in terms of materials, children and time, and see how we can use the child's mental abilities as a means of finding solutions to some organisational problems.

4

Organisation as a thinking activity

During his first weeks in school the child needs to enter a well-established way of life in the classroom. This is guaranteed for him either through the teacher's previous planning, or because he enters the structured and stable community of, for example, a vertically grouped class.

Once the child has discovered what life in school is about and the problems of working amongst many others have impinged on his personal freedom, he is ready to understand some of the simpler principles of organisation and to play an active part in helping to make the classroom workshop a place where each child gets a fair deal. The major job occurs, of course, at the beginning of a new year and the six- and seven-year-old children have sufficient experience to take some responsibility in organising their new class. Subsequent problems can be added to these responsibilities as they arise, with ever-increasing demands being made on even the youngest children as they show themselves ready to participate.

Space is perhaps the simplest problem for the child to deal with. Experience has shown him that although indoor spaces in school are big, the number of children they have to accommodate makes individual space very small. He has also discovered that in order to secure a measure of freedom and movement for himself within a large group of other children, he has to forego the right to full personal freedom.

At the beginning of the autumn term, Miss F delegated the responsibility for organising the classroom to her thirty-six second-year children. 'We will start,' she suggested, 'by making a list of all the activities we want in the classroom.' The children suggested familiar activities, adding a few of their own such as 'A Hospital Corner', and 'Somewhere to keep our own things so's the baby won't get them at home'. Miss F's personal requirement was, 'I need a table for my display. I brought back some stones and olive wood and pottery from my holiday in Greece,' she explained. 'And I've lots of other things to show you and each week I shall make a fresh display.' Together, children and teacher compiled the list of 'corners'.

Miss F then gave each group of children a large sheet of paper. 'That is the classroom floor,' she explained. 'Plan where you are going to put things. Then we shall all know what the classroom will look like before we start.'

Many arguments arose. 'We can't have the paint near the door. The wind blows the paper about when it's open. Besides, we've got to have the paint near the sink for washing the brushes.' 'We want the waste and paste near the paint. Then we can paint the things we've made.' 'We can put the writing table in the reading corner. Then when we need a book it's there.' 'The shop must go near the Wendy House so we can buy the things for making the tea party. . . . Yes. And the dressing-up must be near the Wendy House as well.'

George, the mathematician, interrupted. 'You've drawn them all too small. They take up more room and you won't have space in the middle for building with big bricks.' Eventually, Miss F assembled their suggestions on to a major plan. 'Most of the things we need are in the store cupboard', she had already done some planning ahead. 'You don't all need to do everything, do you?'

George's budding powers of leadership emerged. 'The easels

are big,' he suggested, 'We need some big boys to get the paint corner right.' Mary joined in. 'Our lot,' she indicated six of her small gang of friends, 'will get the shop and the Wendy House open.' Most of the children divided off into groups each with a job and Miss F was left with the unattached to help her with her display corner. These few were either the slower children whose mental powers constantly needed her stimulation, or the divergent whose ideas were rarely conducive to harmony. These were the children who needed to work more closely with her.

Miss B with her class of seven-year-old children hesitated to start from scratch. She arranged the major areas of activity before the term began. Then concentrated on apparatus and small equipment.

'There are six rubber aprons,' she said. 'Where do you think we should keep them?' Some obvious suggestions emerged. 'Near the sink for water and paint and clay,' a number of children suggested. Peter had other ideas. 'We should have them in the cloakroom,' he said. 'Then if we take off our jackets or pullovers when we do paint or clay, we can hang them where they won't get splashed.'

Scissors and pencils were allocated a permanent position. 'Then we can all help to check up and see none's missing.' 'You can put up those hooks for the scissors, Miss B,' was one suggestion. 'And we'll make holes in the lid of this box to stand the pencils up in like you see at the post office.'

Reading apparatus was allocated a space under the window. 'If you want to get it right you have to see it well. Some of those cards are tricky.' Mathematical equipment was required near the waste and paste. 'Then we can get a measure quick for cutting the card the right size and I shan't knock the paint over trying to get to the rulers and things.'

Miss B also delegated the job of making an inventory of available equipment to a group of four, two boys and two girls. 'You can make a stock book,' she said. 'Every Friday you

29

can check it.' Michael, one of the group, added darkly, 'We'll put the prices on as well. Then we'll know how much money we've lost.' Miss B later followed up this lead when ordering fresh apparatus and equipment for the classroom. She discussed the catalogues with the stock-book group and together they made out the fresh order which was sent to the Head Mistress for approval.

As the work develops during the year, children need to group and re-group according to the situation. Many teachers determine these groups themselves, deciding by ability, specific aptitude in a skill, or interest and the like. It's worth experimenting with the notion of letting the children take a hand. This can be done casually, merely by the way in which a particular material or situation attracts a group of children, by natural friendship grouping and the like. Or again the children can be intellectually involved.

'A lot of you want to do things about the street. There won't be time for everybody to do everything. You could make groups.' Again the help of the teacher is needed in establishing some basic system. 'Here's a plan of the street. You've said you want to make the shops, a lighting system, the road with Belisha crossing and cars and lorries, some market stalls and lots of people being busy. How shall we decide who does each of these things?'

Once children have had experience of this kind, they become interested in wider problems of organising groups of people. 'Who says which class we go into?', one little girl wanted to know. 'Do all little boys and girls go to an infants?' another one enquired. Tom had an answer to that. 'No,' he said firmly. 'My cousin Peter is six like I am, and he goes to the same school as Syd and he's nine.'

These children went to the Head Mistress to ask about such mysteries and she explained in simple terms the way in which she organised the school (vertical grouping). 'I know,' Tom recalled. 'On that first day when I came, you told my Mum that all the classes in our school are the same and you can't go up and down, but when we go to the Juniors we'll be with all the eights, or all the nines, or all the tens, or all the elevens.' The children went on to discuss with the Head Mistress why they had mixed groups in the Infant School, and such comments as 'Now we know about school we can help the new ones when they come and show them where we keep all the things' and 'If we always have the same group we get to know everybody and it makes it easy and we can have a lot of things to share', indicated their ability to understand some of the principles behind vertical grouping.

Another aspect of organisation is the arrangement of time during the day, or the week. Time is a difficult concept and remains at a very elementary stage in development during the first year in school. The rhythm of the school day helps to establish a sense of duration and of a sequence of events, and the six- or seven-year-old children are well able to pay attention to it. Time has a particular challenge for the young whose timeless approach to life is so often disrupted because the bell goes, or the teacher says stop and do something else, or the Head Mistress wants us all in the hall.

Children can understand the idea that there are times we must all accept and these can be plotted along a time line. They can then consider how the 'spaces' are to be used. The teacher can claim some part of these spaces for times when she directs activities. The time line is easier to understand than the circle of a clock. It can be clearly laid out along a wall, or if space is short, vertically down a door. If a clock is situated nearby, the children will learn to associate 'Our doing track', as one child called it, with the times as shown by the clock. When the unexpected occurs, as for example the visit of the Safety First official, the children can note the exchange of part of their day for his visit. In a similar way, a shorter session, such as a baking session, can be plotted in advance. 'Twenty minutes for mixing, fifteen minutes for cooking, ten minutes for washing up. That means we need forty-five minutes, or three-quarters of an hour. We must start as soon as we come back from the hall.'

As the children grow older, they can plan their own day to include a number of prescribed activities. In many schools, for example, spontaneous learning is reinforced by simple assignments, and the need to fit in, say, some of the work cards on weighing, time to read a chosen story, written observation of developments on the investigation table etc., can require the child to make for himself a daily timetable. Many children get great satisfaction from plotting their time in this way providing they are not expected to look too far ahead. 'When I write my day out,' Brenda observed, 'I get it all done.'

All of these experiences offer the child opportunities to engage in vigorous mental activity. They have also a powerful part to play in the discipline of the group. When the teacher has delegated responsibility and helped children to take it and understand what responsibility is about, the children impose on themselves a form of self-organisation which is far more effective than discipline from without. Not only do they hold themselves responsible as individuals for leaving an apron where it can be found by the next child, for being aware that in a crowded room you move carefully, etc., but they are mindful of one another. When a group of children are in charge of the 'box of real money', for instance, it is very rare indeed to find any missing. Packets of nuts in the shop only leave it when money is paid for them, missing books get chased home, and Miss X's scissors are always on her desk at the end of the day.

Even clearing away can become a decision-making activity. 'If we want a nice long story time, packing up needs to be done quickly, but it must be done well too. How can we make sure that everything is put where we can find it tomorrow? How many people do we need to sort out the make box? All these boxes must fit under that table. Find the best way of making them all fit in.'

In one school, the staff and Head Mistress had decided to change over to vertical grouping. They realised that the change in organisation would affect not only the teachers but children and parents as well. In this school the Head Mistress decided to discuss the matter with the children even before she met their parents. She planned to send a letter to parents inviting them to discuss her plans for reorganisation during the same week in which the plans were put to the children in school.

The six- and seven-year-old children she approached herself. She started by asking them about the existing mode of organisation and was surprised by their knowledge and understanding. One child gave her the lead she needed. 'Why does it have to be all sixes or sevens together?' he asked. 'It isn't like that at home. I've got a friend who lives next door to me. He's in Miss J's class and I can play with him at home.'

The Head Mistress followed this up by explaining the way in which the new classes would be formed. Then she added, 'When all the classes have different ages together in them, we shall be able to work with people in another classroom some- times, because every classroom will have books and games and things for all the different ages.'

The older children were delighted and excited by the ideas she put to them. When her letters reached home, these children were ready to convey a favourable opinion to their parents, even before she met them. They also passed on the ideas to the younger children who had been told a little about the change by their teachers. Generally, the younger children seemed to show little interest, although one five-year-old took home the message, 'There won't be a baby class any more in our school, and if we want to play with Meccano we can.'

By the time the organisational changes were made in this school the staff had the unanimous support of children and parents, and were able to deal successfully with the inevitable problems and disappointments which accompany any major change.

Experience of organisation helps the child to become more aware of the fundamental order behind the universe. The eggs take twenty-eight days to hatch. The tree takes a full year to complete its cycle. Night and day succeed one another with amazing regularity, and the child begins to feel he belongs to a wondrously ordered universe. Through his own attempts to order his life he feels linked with the miraculous order of total existence. The next chapter will deal with the child's developing awareness of the universal pattern in which he has been allotted a unique role.

5

Movement and mental activity

Movement makes life what it is. Without movement there would be no life. Basic to living is the process of learning, and without movement no learning takes place.

The child moves before it is born. From the moment of birth movement never ceases. Even during deep sleep some movement continues, and when the child is awake vigorous activity is one of his greatest needs.

In the early days of life movement of the body is a total experience. This undifferentiated movement is highly eloquent of the baby's physical and psychological state. As he grows older, he learns to differentiate, control and co-ordinate his movements. He learns to move a single specified part of his body and to move two or more parts in unison.

Even in the days of rigidly formal education, the child's need to move was provided for, but usually for only a short period daily, and many teachers can remember the burst of unleashed energy during play-time breaks. Movement was seen as a means of 'letting off steam' and a certain amount of it kept the body healthy. The emphasis today is on the contribution of vigorous activity to the physical and psychological well-being of the individual, but are we sufficiently aware of the part it plays in the mental life of the child? Study the index of most books on primary education. Physical activity is usually included, but where is it placed in the order of priorities? How far do we really see the movement of the child for what it is?

Young teachers soon discover the importance of professional competence in physical education. In the early days of their career, relationships with a group of children are often made, or destroyed, in the physical education lesson. The urgent need of the child for adequate physical activity is so important to him that he will tolerate many inadequacies on the part of his teacher if she can satisfy his deep-seated urge to move.

As we watch the growing infant we are made aware that movement is much more than a physical need. That force which drives him forward with such a sense of purpose has far deeper roots in his being.

In his earlier days the child must learn without words, and learning depends largely on himself. He faces the vast unknown with a burning curiosity which sets him searching for information. He explores with his hands, his eyes and his ears, but primarily it is through his sense of touch that all he encounters becomes familiar. The wider the scope for skin contact, the more information he receives, and as his mobility increases, so his world expands. The child whose horizon is bound by the play-pen, who is strapped in a high chair, or kept quiet, has little opportunity to make his discoveries and learning is restricted.

Charles had a problem which is typical of many only children. Mother and Father were at work all day, and from the age of eighteen months Charles was left with a kindly, but ageing, neighbour. To her way of thinking, she looked after him well. He had a good midday meal and an afternoon sleep. She showed him picture books which he loved and kept a good store of simple constructional toys with which he could play on the table attached to his chair. When his mother fetched him at night, he was always clean and tidy and often ready to go straight to bed, 'so that Mother could prepare the evening meal'.

By the time Charles was two and a half he had gained a lot of weight and his height was normal, but he was obviously not developing his motor skills as he should and he began to whimper quite a lot. One day he was whimpering when Mother came to fetch him and the neighbour looked upset. 'He seems to be losing interest,' she complained, 'in the things I give to him. I'm sure he has all he needs, and I never let him get into any kind of danger. I don't understand it.'

In protecting him from danger she was also restricting his activity to a point which inhibited learning. He had discovered what he could from the toys he was offered and so they no longer motivated him.

A few weeks later, a play-group opened in the neighbourhood and Mother registered Charles. 'It will give you a rest,' she said to the kindly neighbour. Within weeks, Charles was competing with other active toddlers, sometimes coming home dirty and often very untidy, but he no longer whimpered. He chattered in great excitement about the things he made with large packing cases, car tyres and planks of wood. His movements became much more vigorous and co-ordinated and so did his mind.

Studies of the development of early thinking emphasise the significance of sensory-motor learning in the first years of life. At first objects exist for the child only through what he does with them. Physical impressions are assimilated and give rise to mental images. By the time the child is two or three he is well able to recall an image of a familiar object, even when the object is no longer present, but he would never do so unless he had manipulated the object. He learns to perceive relationships by moving objects about, and moving himself from place to place. What he learns to manipulate with his hands he will later be able to manipulate in thought.

The impressions he forms and retains as a result of his actions enable the child to construct a mental model of his world. With his hands he explores the shape of his own body and eventually identifies himself as a separate entity. At first he places himself at the centre of his simple mental model and relates to himself various bits of the pattern as he discovers them. Gradually his manipulations lead him to understand that there are other points of view and that he is a very small piece in an immense complicated pattern. He can pinch his own toe and he feels a pain. If he pinches his mother's nose, he can't feel the pain, but it is obvious to him that *she* can. By moving from point to point, by moving objects about, his general mental map becomes established and provides a framework to which he can attach other ideas. As he matures and increases the number and range of his experiences, he accumulates a vast array of impressions which are inter-related. His powers of mental manipulation improve and early patterns of thought begin to emerge.

Before the child can progress to a stage of logical reasoning, he must learn to perform certain fundamental thought activities.

The first of these is the notion of invariance. It is through his own actions that the child learns about the permanence of objects. He learns about the hardness of the wooden table by banging it and poking it and grasping its legs in his hands. Each time he performs these operations he makes the same discovery. The information he has obtained is confirmed time and time again, until its invariant nature makes it thoroughly predictable.

This notion of the permanence of objects gradually expands to include the permanence of the bulk, or amount, of matter. Continuous substances such as water or oil, and collections of discrete objects such as particles of sand, beads, pills, etc. behave in a correspondingly conservative way: that is, the amount remains unchanged irrespective of the way in which it is distributed or divided.

The toddler who spills water from a small cup on to the floor sees it spread to cover a very great area. If the sand in his bucket is wet it stays piled in a compact pie, while the same quantity of dry sand would spread out to form a wide heap. He will do these things many times before he understands that, in spite of what his eyes tell him, the quantity doesn't change.

Even at the age of six and a half this notion of the conservation of matter may not be confirmed. Peter, who is nearly seven, still thinks that he has more bricks when they're scattered across the floor than he has when he's packed them back in the box. The physical experience of packing the bricks into the box will help to establish the fact that their number doesn't change, but only when he has reached a certain stage in cognitive development will Peter accept the notion completely.

The second thought process fundamental to reasoning is the notion of reversibility, the idea that by reversing a process we move back to the original starting point. Again it is through physical manipulation that the child learns that this is so. We may try to reassure the five-year-old by telling him that he will have the original six toy cars in his garage when the two he has lent the visitor to play with are restored, but he will remain unconvinced until he has actually pushed them back into the garage. This and similar operations will be performed many times, awaiting the stage when his thought processes are mature enough to hold and use the idea behind the actions his muscles perform.

These and many other mental activities grow out of the physical movements of the child. He will not learn them through verbal explanation, and the child who is kept still for most of his working hours, or whose powers of locomotion are restricted, has little opportunity to develop adequate patterns of thought, and his ultimate mental structures will have insecure foundations. He must move in order to learn how to think.

A two-year-old accompanied her parents on a full-day bus

tour of exciting countryside. When things were pointed out
to her she smiled obligingly, and when passengers alighted
from the bus she stood quietly beside her parents, or followed
them obediently along the river bank, or sea-shore. Not once
during the whole journey did she squeal or show any inclina-
tion to climb or explore. Towards the end of the journey,
other adults on the bus congratulated the parents on having
such a lovely child. 'I've never seen a child so young who
could be good like that for a whole day,' they said.

The parents were delighted and the child basked in adult
approval. If she continues to respond in this way to such
approval, what will be the outcome?

The situation was worrying for at least two reasons. A
child so young should not be exposed, unless it is strictly
necessary, to such an unnatural environment for so long at a
stretch. Nor should she be subject to the pressure of adult
approval for such docile behaviour. The adults were no more
disturbed than if there had not been a child amongst them,
and the child had learned no more from the experience than
how to be good and so please the adults. What she could have
gained in experience from river and shore and mountain
forest was lost opportunity.

In his natural state, the child makes use of his natural
environment as a source of physical and mental challenge.
Wide-open spaces, or shore, or countryside, trees and rocks,
rivers and thundering waves, exercise the child's powers of
mobility and offer him scope for developing ideas about
space and shape and balance, and the relationship between
physical objects.

We bring him into school because society has decided he
must learn the arts and skills of his social group. We offer him
substitutes for his naturally challenging environment. The
large hall, the playground, the fields and the climbing frame
and play apparatus are good attempts on our part, but they
have many limitations, and there is much the teacher must

do if the child is to be compensated physically and mentally. In all circumstances the adult can help the child to explore and expand his growing knowledge of physical activity and the intellectual impressions he gains from it.

When children first enter school they may know the major parts of the body, but they may not know all the names of the parts and few of them know how the parts work. The child's body itself provides an excellent visual aid. He can see, move and name each part, he can observe for himself how his bones are linked together and how his muscles control his limbs.

As soon as Lisa showed an interest in her fingers and toes, her mother started to play the naming game. 'This is Lisa's toe', 'This is Lisa's nose', etc. Lisa loved the game and soon added the idea. 'Lisa nose . . . Mummy nose . . . Lisa foot . . . Mummy foot . . .,' etc.

Lisa remained intensely interested in the parts of her body she could name. When she heard music, she waved her arms and fluttered her fingers and watched them as though fascinated. By the time she came into school her movements were beautifully co-ordinated and she wanted to know 'What makes my hand move by itself?' (i.e. while the rest of her body stayed still). Simple explanations to questions of this kind increased Lisa's sense of bodily awareness, and throughout her early years, movement remained her most eloquent mode of communication. She invariably expressed her feelings and reactions through the way she moved.

The child's movement vocabulary forms an important part of his learning. Modern approaches to dance are designed round the exploration of the movement of the body in space, the rate of movement and the strength of it. A child of five may understand fast and slow, but there is much he has to learn about faster, not so fast as, faster than, etc., and then about associated ideas such as swift, rushing, hurrying, scurrying, hurtling and so on. Rate of movement contains

41

some difficult ideas for the child to grasp. Rate is related to time, which is a complicated and difficult concept. The child of two can kick a ball, but he will be three or four before he can catch one, mainly because his sense of timing is un-developed.

A child of three may be aware of different degrees of strength in movement. At this stage his knowledge of move-ment may be ahead of his vocabulary. He will respond to such words as 'tip-toe', or 'stamp', but not to 'light', or 'heavy'. Introducing these words and linking them with his respective movements will help him to understand the new words and add them to his vocabulary. There are a great many words, even those of a more abstract nature such as 'smooth', 'immediately', or 'gently', which acquire meaning for the child through his own bodily experiences.

There are many important ideas about space and shape which emerge from the child's physical activities. To begin with his body is a small, but interesting shape, in a large space. Each of the many shapes which go to make his body can be moved and as a result his body can make many different shapes. When he learns to work with a partner, or in a group, the range of these shapes is vastly increased.

Each part of the child's body is unique in shape and the shape of it is designed to fulfil a particular purpose. The economy in design of the body is a miracle of perfection. The shape of hands or limbs, and the way in which they perform their tasks interest the five- and six-year olds, while a seven-year-old child often becomes interested in more intricate shapes, such as the ear or eye.

Steve was slightly deaf. When he was first equipped with a hearing aid, he became suddenly conscious of his handicap and rather unhappy because he had to wear an aid. His teacher told him, 'It's a very clever little box. Shall I show you how it works?' With the aid of a model ear she showed Steve the part his aid had to play. Steve became very excited and anxious to pass on the information to his friends. His hearing aid was now a source of interest rather than an embarrassment, and he no longer felt handicapped.

We live in an age when space is at a premium and many young children have little experience of unrestricted space. The school hall may be their first adventure in a large indoor space. Many reception class teachers find that children 'go mad' when introduced to a hall for the first time. Some children are afraid of such unusual freedom.

'Mark hides under my desk,' Mrs Y explained, 'every time he knows we're going into the big hall. It doesn't matter whether it's service time when the whole school assembles, or whether it's movement, with just my own class.'

Mark was an intelligent little boy and when he lost some of his apprehension, he could talk about his feelings '—don't know what to do with it all,' he said.

The child's exploration of space in a hall usually follows a definite pattern. At first a group of children tend to run round and round in an anti-clockwise direction, often shrieking and falling about. The advice of the teacher to 'use up the corners' may go over their heads, for in their topological view, a hall is bound by a wall which simply 'goes all round'. 'Find a space and sit in it', 'Stand where you can't touch anyone else', etc. may be more effective.

As Mark knew, there is much a child needs to do with space before he can come to terms with it and understand the relationships between himself and space, and other people and objects in the same space.

In adult life, understanding of spatial relationships varies considerably between individuals. An inner sense of how pieces of a pattern fit on to material, of how items of furniture can be arranged in a room, of whether the car will manoeuvre into a parking lot, comes to us from experience of the concrete situation. Children who have plenty of scope for manipulating objects in space of all sizes gain a foundational knowledge and

43

the mathematical implications are enormous. Tidying the play house, fitting equipment into boxes, returning physical education apparatus to its corner, are all useful experiences in this respect.

With the help of the teacher, children can become more consciously aware of movement problems and learn habits of dealing with them in everyday life. 'Stand tall for a minute and look,' Mrs W advised Ben who wanted to reach the book corner at the other side of the room. 'Which is the best way to get to the books without upsetting anyone else?' Thus called upon, Ben noticed that a straight line wasn't the best, or quickest route.

As the child gains control over bodily movement he grows more and more aware of rhythm. Movement follows a pattern with emphasis in different places. The skill of the hurdler running and leaping depends on establishing an economical rhythmic pattern. Working movements, such as hammering and sawing, or sewing, or beating cake mixture, have the rhythm of light and shade. Organic movements in the body such as breathing and the beating of the heart are bound by rhythm. Indeed the rhythm of such movements indicates whether things are right or wrong.

Children can be helped to observe these rhythms; to beat out, for instance, the rhythm of hopping or skipping. They can observe one another and compare rhythmic patterns of movement. Later they can match their movements to a pre-scribed rhythm, but many children of six or seven experience great difficulty in matching movements of their own body to the rhythm of a piece of music.

The total movement of the young child gradually gives way to increased skill in selective movement of isolated parts of the body. The seven-year-old may watch his own hands prescribing intricate shapes and patterns. The adult can help him to become equally aware of the movements of his feet, of a leg, of his shoulder blades, or of his head.

Facial movement is equally fascinating and is an essential part of communication. The young child has far fewer words than the adult and depends on movements of the body and the face to express and communicate impressions. 'There's a thing in the garden and I don't know what it is. It's as big as this. . . . It's sort of round like this . . . with spiky things here and here and here. . . . And when it's awake it looks like this . . . and it moves like this. . . .' Vivid impressions can be communicated using very few words. The observant adult may learn more about a child and his reactions to events by watching his movements, than by talking to him.

At this stage a study of how things move is of great interest to a child. Living things grow, lever and haul themselves along the ground; they lever their way through water, or through the air. The same basic principles are applied in any medium through which movement takes place. Man levers himself along when he walks. He can also roll or haul. Levering, rolling and hauling are principles applied in technology and the child can observe these principles in many situations.

The tail of a fish, the wing of a pigeon, the ribs of a snake, rollers under the pyramid stones, ball-bearings, wheels on roller-skates and the pulley-block of a crane, are exciting examples of locomotion, and there is much a child can learn from them by close observation.

After watching a television programme, six-year-old children described jet propulsion as 'Thrusting away by pushing hard at something behind'. When movement principles are introduced in simple form, children are perfectly capable of grasping them.

How people move is another source of interest. The bricklayer, the painter and the baker use movements which are characteristic of their job. Children in their spontaneous dramatic play may imitate the movements of the refuse collector, of the bus conductor, or the policeman on points duty. These movements are purposeful, effective and economical. Why people move as they do makes a worthwhile study which will challenge thought and careful observation on the part of the child.

An important aspect of movement is keeping still. Many children, if asked to sit, lie or stand still impose rigid restrictions on bodily movement which result in tension, and tension is full of small movements of the muscles. Children can learn to let movement go rather than hold themselves still and so learn to relax the whole body and, later, some particular part of it.

Even in the dark, or at a distance, we can usually identify a familiar person by the way he moves. Movement of the body, of the emotions, of the imagination has in the course of a lifetime helped to create a person's mind. Through movement, interaction between external and internal worlds takes place, and through movement each continues to modify the other. What a person becomes is echoed in the shape of himself and in how that shape uses space. Just as no two people look exactly alike, so no two people move exactly alike.

By helping the child to become more fully aware of his own movement and the movements of others, we help him to improve his powers of learning. The world is full of movement and the child moving in his world can learn to understand his role in the ever-changing pattern of a kaleidoscopic universe.

6

A thinking approach to literacy

Literacy means the ability to write as well as read, and attention will be paid in this chapter to the quality of mental activity demanded of the young learner in the process of becoming literate. Teachers employ a number of approaches to the teaching of literacy, and we shall examine some of these with a view to evaluating differences in quality between them.

The traditional focus in the education of young children is on reading, writing and number, and it has usually been assumed that the development of skill in these can in itself foster intellectual growth. How far it does has never been determined. In any event, teachers have two alternatives; they can select procedures which help the child to develop a skill and offer him intellectual challenge, or they can help him to acquire a skill in a superficial way, while remaining virtually unconcerned about the growth of his mind.

Language can be used as a means of feeding the child with facts which he is expected to memorise, or it can be used as a means of helping the child to clarify and express ideas he had formulated himself. By comparison with original thinking, memorising is an impoverished quality of the mind. In any sphere, learning which requires the child to think for himself is far superior to the type of mini-learning which depends basically on memorising. When the child has sufficient personal experience to which the experience of others can be attached, reading and writing become a major means of imparting and articulating knowledge. In the early stages it is highly important for learning to be a thinking, rather than a mere memorising, process, for the use a person makes of knowledge is the reason for acquiring it. How he uses knowledge depends on the quality of thought he brings to the acquisition of it.

Each of the following Infant Schools is successful in helping children to acquire an appropriate level of skill in their ability to read and write before they transfer to the Junior School.

School A, using 'Janet and John' as a basic scheme, adopts an approach which combines 'look and say' and 'phonics'. Books outside the scheme are also used to widen interest in reading, and the child's own experiences form the basis of his written work. Systematic tuition in reading starts in the reception class and here the teacher's aim is to familiarise the child with the basic words of the Introductory Books. Flash cards are her main material and she devises an ingenious array of word games which confirm the child's sight vocabulary before he is introduced to a reading book. Children then proceed from book to book in the scheme. With the aid of mothers, who join the classes for an hour or two each day, teachers hear every child read every day and his progress through the scheme is indicated on his individual book marker.

Copy writing is introduced alongside early reading games. The child first practises making balls and sticks in a variety of media such as paint, crayon, chalk and Plasticine. He then graduates to copying words from the flash cards. Eventually he completes a page of News each day by copying into his News Book a simple sentence he has watched the teacher write for the group. As soon as he can do this successfully, he is encouraged to make his own sentences and is given a number of beginnings such as 'I can see a . . .', 'This is my . . .', 'Here is a . . .' to help him.

In School B, reading and writing are taught simultaneously. A wealth of inviting books are available, while 'Time for Reading' is used as a basic scheme because it is attractive, employs a combination of methods, enables the teacher to teach phonic work systematically while taking advantage of incidental opportunities for reading and writing which arise from the child's various activities. This scheme also includes a number of work-books which associate reading with kinaesthetic learning. These work-books, along with other apparatus and games, provide appropriate reading activities for a large number of children, leaving the teacher free to listen to children read. Imaginative stories offer plenty of scope for oral and written language work, and the apparatus and materials are designed to combine the development of reading and writing skills. An important adjunct to the scheme is the teacher's manual, which is particularly helpful in the guidance it offers inexperienced teachers. School B feels that by using this approach their children get the best of both worlds, a combination of spontaneous exploration of the written and printed word through interest, and the guidance of a well-planned scheme.

School C links a language-experience approach with an elementary study of language. The teachers in this school are interested in psycho-linguistics because they feel that both they and the children should know not only how to use the mother tongue, but something of the nature and structure of language itself. They see reading as a means of obtaining meaning from the printed word and believe that the search for meaning should predominate in all reading experiences. They also believe that, in the first stages, children should learn to read primarily from their own vocabulary, that they should learn to understand some of the rules which govern language patterns as they acquire literary skills, and that developing skill with written language should grow from the study of the printed code.

Teachers in School C are familiar with the many sub-skills required of the child when reading, and with the higher skills which later form part of the continuous process of reading development. At all stages they try to involve the child in conscious mental activity, and his attention is drawn to such language skills as he can understand. The invariance of letter or word shapes, for example, is a concept the child needs to develop before he can make confident progress. The fact that everything ever written in the English language is created by rearrangement of twenty-six basic patterns is not obvious to the beginner. He can be helped to recognise that the same words are used over and over again, that the twenty-six adopted symbols may vary slightly in appearance without changing fundamentally in pattern. This idea of invariance is not unique to reading. It is a fundamental concept in all aspects of learning. Calculation depends on the invariant nature of numbers. Composition of music depends on the invariance of notes. The arrangement of furniture in a room depends on the invariance of individual pieces of furniture and the relationship they bear to one another and so on.

School C uses 'Breakthrough' sentences and word-making material as an aid to reading and writing. The teachers do not depend on a basic reading scheme. The emphasis throughout is on a study of words, of how each word is made and of ways in which words are put together and used. Reading and writing, in this school, are only a part of a vast complex of language activities.

Each of these schools considers itself to be progressive in approach and outlook, and each claims to obtain a highly acceptable level of literacy at every stage. We need to look behind the ability of the children to read fluently from a simple text and to write a few comprehensible sentences in order to reveal the real quality of the work.

The flash card approach employed in School A centres round developing the child's visual memory. Correct response to visual stimulation is rewarded by the approval of the teacher and of the group and, later, by being given a reading book. Progress is checked against the child's sight vocabulary, and the main motivation lies in proceeding to the next stage, or book. Writing development is also a matter of memorising and reproducing a few correct patterns. Rarely is the child required to think beyond recalling the right response. At the end of the process he has learned to 'read' and to 'write' without making any real mental effort. In other words, he has acquired social skills with a minimum of intellectual growth. The child who can follow the rules excels in this approach and may even score higher than the intelligent child who prefers to know the reasons behind the works.

In School B certainly more demand is made on the child. He is motivated largely through interest, and involved in the process through his muscles and senses. He should emerge with skill enough to enjoy reading and so find reading a meaningful pursuit. He could very well learn good habits of reading and writing, and be sufficiently interested in doing these things to carry on doing them in adult life.

We must turn to School C, however, before we are made aware that the child's literary development offers far greater possibilities than the adequate acquisition of skills. The children are being encouraged to think about what they are doing and to develop intellectual powers which are of far greater importance than mere good learning habits.

There is a stage in the child's cognitive development when stimulus-response learning plays an important role, but children of school age have normally passed this stage, and the way they are taught should be geared to the stage they *have* reached in intellectual growth.

By the time the child enters school he is familiar with many types of symbols. At the nursery stages, indeed, symbolism forms the core of much of his play. The play bricks serve equally well as letters in the postman's bag, sweets in a jar, corned-beef dinner on a plate, or units in construction. Many five-year-olds know that pictures and printed words are symbols, and that they tell the 'reader' about the real thing. At this stage they can be helped to understand the invariance of symbols, that whenever you see the word 'John', for instance, it always stands for the name 'John'. In their early pictures, children themselves adopt standardised symbols to represent the sun, a house, a man, a tree, etc. Their minds are prepared to accept the invariance of the printed code.

By the end of the first year in school the child's powers of classification are well advanced. He enjoys sorting and assembling objects which are alike. He depends a great deal on visual information and may be able to identify similar words, or words that start or end in the same way, by visual pattern. His powers of auditory discrimination may be less well developed and he may be unable to benefit from work with phonics which depends very much on the development of auditory skills. He may need to wait a little longer before phonic work can be of use to him.

Many of our children remain at the intuitive stage of thinking throughout the Infant School. They can repeat a sequence of sounds, e.g. 'm' 'a' 'n', and yet fail to understand these sounds as clues to a word. They may make a bright guess, e.g. 'bloke', which in their mode of speech, may fit the situation, but the breaking down and reassembling of sounds in words is beyond their powers of comprehension, because they have not yet developed the notion of reversibility.

During the last year in the Infant School, many children enter a stage of concrete operational thinking. They begin to think and reason through the concrete situation. Mental operations take place as a result of what they do. Moreover, they have reached a stage when their thoughts are reversible and they understand the invariance of matter. It is at this stage that material such as 'Breakthrough', which can be easily manipulated, is most useful. The child who has made sense by putting self-chosen words in the right order, knows something about a sentence and what to expect when he meets sentences which have been composed by others.

At six-and-a-half Tony had a sight vocabulary of about 100 words. When asked to read, 'Peter saw the big red bus', he read 'Peter was the big red bus', and it didn't worry him in the least that what he read didn't make sense. Two months later, he made a similar mistake, then stopped and laughed: 'No. It can't be that,' he said. 'That doesn't say the right thing.' Tony understood by now what to expect of a sentence and had developed the ability to perceive the significance of the order of letters in a word.

The acquisition of sub-skills in reading is closely related to stages of mental growth, and teachers who can identify these sub-skills, and introduce experience of them at the right time, are teaching effectively and with economy.

The one-to-one correspondence, for instance, between spoken and written words may not be apparent to the five-year-old, who hears much of what is said to him as prolonged patterns of sound. The need to follow from left to right and from the top of the page to the bottom, may be understood by the six-year-old who has shared a book with adults. Even so, he may still have to learn to view all words from left to right before he can obtain sound clues from them, and he may still be a little uncertain of exactly what a word is.

Six-year-old Mike waved his book excitedly at a sympathetic visitor to his class, 'I've got the orange book,' he said. The visitor, thinking he wanted to demonstrate his skill to her, said, 'You must be a good reader, then. Would you like to read to me?' Mike brushed the offer aside. His excitement

53

mounted. 'I've got the orange book,' he repeated. 'And do you know, it's got the same words in it.' Mike, a sensible little boy, had only just discovered that in reading we use the same words over and over again, and that he need not learn a whole new set when he opened a fresh book.

An essential factor in reading and writing is the content of the matter with which the child is asked to deal. Reading schemes are improving and more attention has been paid to content in recently published schemes. Yet there is still much which is trite and unrealistic. Even the better schemes tend to remain tied to the trivial domestic scene in home and classroom, and there is a great need for imaginative and challenging literature for the introductory stages of reading. The author who, from a limited vocabulary, can create humour and excitement would be welcome by any publisher.

While the emphasis remains on the mechanics of decoding rather than on obtaining the message, reading will be taught by stimulus-response modes of learning which make little intellectual demand on the child. The child's introduction to print can affect the way he feels about it for the rest of his life. When teachers and publishers really understand what reading is about, then children will be respected and so offered reading material of literary worth which fires the imagination and exercises the mind.

Once the child, through the use of his own words, has developed the basic concepts of reading, he needs content which will expand his universe and whisk him away on wings of imagery and imagination into exciting situations which exercise his ability to think. This surely is one of the main incentives to read, to be shown unexplored aspects of life and given access to fabulous worlds. What purpose is there in learning to read if your efforts don't lead you up and out?

And what purpose is there in learning to write unless it is to commit something worth saying to paper? Reading through a set of work-cards intended to provide an introduction to writing the English language makes one wonder why the child ever bothers. Obviously in his early efforts the child is bound by the words with which he is familiar, but he can be helped to use his familiar words in interesting ways; it is the skill and sensitivity of the adult who teaches him, rather than the unknown author of language exercises, who is able to give him this help.

The idea of castles fired Jonathan's imagination. He asked many questions and eventually assembled his limited store of historical facts and created the scene for himself.

'Once upon a time,' he wrote, 'a man called Sir William Walter bilt his castle in 1884 inside is an old piece of furniture it is a box full of jewels in the cellar in the olden days they used to burn logs. In stead of nice chairs they had wuden chairs instead of cookers they had a stove they had a golden statue the flor was paved in gold the worls were paved in silver the table was in wood with a thread of gold and silver plates with silver food dishes ther wer glasers insted of cups the tea pot was made out of gold the little cuberd had some silver and gold cups on top of a little table wer an fabulous ornament it was a Bull on an gold island and the wall had a lot of corvings of stone 3 swords was on the wall In sted of woshers a tub was required with a wobbly board they just rub the clowes up and doan the bath was a tub insted of taps they had to put weter in a bucet. the end.'

Children try to grapple with quite difficult concepts and we are often surprised by their understanding when we encourage them to express it. A number of children aged four to seven were asked, 'What is reading?' and 'Why do you learn to read?' Apart from a few children who said, 'Don't know' to both questions, the replies of others varied widely, and each child gave a considered response. 'Reading,' said a six-year-old, 'is opening and shutting your mouth.' 'Words in a book,' said another. A seven-year-old said, 'What the book says; the sounds', while 'It makes you talk out loud . . . and think', came from a little girl of four. One thoughtful young man scowled; 'That's a very difficult question,' he said. 'I will think about it.'

Answers to the second question came more readily. 'To get clever and pass exams,' was popular, and so was 'Because I have to.' A six-year-old who was struggling with his writing, suggested, 'To know what someone else writes down'. Two little girls from literate homes said. 'Auntie gives me nice books and I want them to tell me stories,' and 'So's I'll be able to read stories to my little girl.' The last comment came from a four-year-old beginner, 'because we like it'.

It is clear from these comments that fundamental concepts in reading were already developing. With no prompting from adults, these children had puzzled out for themselves ideas about procedures which interested them. They needed little encouragement to express their shaping ideas and continued the discussion long after the questions had been asked. The boy who had asked for time to think, eventually contributed, 'Reading is looking at words written down and then saying them.' He paused for a moment, still not satisfied. Then he added, 'But you have to think about what the words say as well.'

Children know that the purpose of reading is to obtain meaning from the printed word and that what is worth reading makes you think. Even in the earliest stages of using decoding skill, children struggle to make sense of material which often has no sense. What can they make, for instance, of the passages of repetitive jargon which form the introductory pages of many reading schemes? Who can blame the child if he loses interest in making the effort?

One young man was given a word recognition test by his teacher. He stared hard at the list of words but made no response to her encouragement. 'I know you know these words,' she urged. The boy shook his head. 'I don't know what they're talking about,' he murmured eventually.

Reading tuition which depends on memorising visual patterns may produce results up to a certain level, but if we wish our children to become truly literate, we must help them to acquire their skills in a thoroughly meaningful way.

7

A thinking approach to numeracy

Long before the child can handle definite mathematical ideas, he senses a growing respect for order and for the clearly definable pattern at the roots of his daily life. He feels urged to distinguish between this and that, to assemble the things which go together, to impose a stable and invariant pattern on the confusion of impressions which impinge upon him.

The child's own inner love of order renders him sensitive to the underlying control which orders the universe. He becomes aware of the unchanging sequence of events between one sunrise and the next, or between successive birthdays. He grows to appreciate the repetitive cycle of natural phenomena. He notices how the cracks in the pavement meet precisely, how each corner of the big table is exactly the same as the other three, how things go together in fours, or twos, or threes. He discovers a magic in individual numbers and may even become obsessed for a while by the need to find his favourite number in each personal experience. At the age of four, Janet favoured the number four, and in many things she did she needed to find four, 'Because,' as she explained with enigmatic logic, 'that makes it one at each corner and then it will be all right.'

Eventually the magnificent idea emerges. There are thoughts in the mind which explain how bits of the universe fit together, thoughts which properly used guarantee that events will turn out as predicted, in much the same way as man calculates a journey into space and a safe return. The threatening world becomes a friendly place when the human mind is in control of it.

Such safeguarding influences border on the divine, and number and superstition are frequently fused. Respect and awe add great excitement to numbers and there is a promise in the wonderful world of ordered ideas. The child discovers these delights for himself long before the adult intervenes and tries to link numbering with memorising. At the age of four, Nicholas finds great excitement in numbers. He has a store of games he has personally invented. 'How many plastic eggs under the dolly's teacup?', for instance, is a game which goes on for hours when he finds a willing partner.

The study of mathematics is frequently equated with intellectual activity, and it is often assumed that the inclusion of mathematics in a school syllabus guarantees mental activity of good quality for the child. In practice, the content of many a school syllabus can be covered in a mode so intellectually undemanding as to make little lasting impression on the child's mind. In this chapter we shall examine the difference between the mere acquisition of mathematical facts and procedures, and the creative growth of mathematical understanding.

A group of students on a mathematics course set out to identify the various ways in which numbers are used in a variety of familiar environments such as the kitchen, a classroom, a garden and a street. Their survey revealed the startling fact that numbers were used far more frequently in many out of school situations, than in the average classroom. The kitchen came high on the list, and, in fact, it became clear that most young children encounter number and mathematical ideas more frequently in the kitchen at home than in any other place. Fundamental ideas about matter and quantity, about measurement and time, about space and shape, about size, proportion, balance and symmetry are freely available to the child in his home. Where an understanding parent is ready to share the child's elementary impressions, good foundations are laid.

The cupboard under the sink in Peter's home is not very big. Peter is three and he enjoys helping his mother by putting away the clean cooking pans. At first he pushes them in at random and finds he can't close the door. Peter's mother is patient. 'Try putting the big pans in first,' she suggests. 'I always put the frying pan at the bottom.' Peter tries a number of times and eventually the door will close. The number of abortive attempts reduces each day, and by the end of the week Peter proudly declares, 'The pans are good today. Look! They're all in and I can close the door.' During the week, Peter's ideas about the way in which parts of space fit together has vastly improved.

Judith is four. Her mother is fond of dressmaking, and Judith hands Mother the pins as she lays out the pattern on the folded material. Judith looks at the shape of the pattern. 'Why are you only making a bit of a dress?' she asks in a puzzled tone. 'I'm cutting two sides of the dress at the same time. The material is folded,' Mother explains. 'See. We'll make a pattern of a dress for your dolly. We do it like this and make two sides the same with the fold going down the middle. Here's some coloured paper. You can cut out a dress with your pattern in coloured paper. Then, if it fits your dolly, you can have these pieces left from my dress and cut dolly a dress like mine.' Within the next few weeks, Judith's dolly acquired a magnificent wardrobe and Judith's ideas of symmetry, of scale and of the relationship between shapes were beginning to form.

In situations such as these mathematical ideas are discovered and the roots of understanding begin to take hold in the young child's mind. Even the less favourable home background contains good mathematical opportunity. Indeed, some children from underprivileged homes, where food and materials are scarce and must be carefully shared, where space is at a premium and must be used sparingly, where money is short and must be carefully budgeted, may develop good mathematical concepts before they acquire linguistic skill.

Steve shopped for his mother from the age of four, and he knew his coins well. There was little enough in Steve's home to go round and he knew how to cut a small cake into three equal portions for himself and two younger siblings. 'They has to be the same,' he explained. 'Then it's fair. Them three bits is all the same.' Steve didn't know the term 'one third', but his idea of fractions was already well founded.

When children first enter school, the problem for the teacher is not so much that of awakening an interest in mathematics, as of using and developing the intense interest already possessed by them. Preparation for her job begins with a study of the mathematical situations the child has already experienced during his pre-school years. In our technological society, children are brought up in a world where mathematics is important. In school the mathematics syllabus must be built round the everyday situations in which the child first meets mathematical challenge.

The personal need to use mathematics arises in a great variety of circumstances. Two-year-old Prue was given a pull-along toy duck at Christmas. A puppy chewed the string through, but big brother Mike, aged five, came gallantly to the rescue. 'I've got some string. Lots of string,' he reassured Prue. 'It only wants a new string.' In a generous mood, he fastened the whole of a five-metre length to Prue's duck and set her a seemingly hopeless problem. Eventually Prue burst into tears and Mike was then faced with the two-fold problem of pacifying her and making the toy work. Trial and error taught him that an adequate length was far more effective than all the string in his pocket, and that to use all you had and hope for the best was by no means the right solution to the problem.

Six-year-old John studied his image in a pier-glass. He moved close to the glass, then withdrew to a distance. He repeated his actions and finally asked. 'If the mirror is only as wide as this (twenty centimetres) how is it I can see all of myself?'

Adrian was making a book about ships. He found some pictures of liners and tried to copy them. Eventually he turned to his teacher in great distress. 'I've tried and tried,' he complained, 'but my ships won't look right.' His teacher showed him how to construct a simple grid and use it as a guide to getting the shape of the ships in proportion.

A group of children decided to rearrange the classroom to simulate a fair-ground. This interest, sparked off by a visiting fair in the vicinity of the school, caught the imagination of the whole class. 'We'll draw the room first,' they planned. 'Then we can think where to put things before we start.' They drew a plan of the classroom, then cut out furniture shapes which they moved about on the plan. Satisfied with their arrangement, they tried to move the furniture about the room. 'It won't fit in like it does on the plan,' they discovered. 'We didn't get the right sizes when we drew it.' They welcomed their teacher's help in scaling down the furniture and estimating the relationships between shapes drawn on the plan.

'I threw a huge crust of bread on the lawn this morning,' Linda exclaimed. 'And a little tiny sparrow gobbled it all up. He ate more than himself.' She discussed the situation with her teacher who suggested, 'It would be difficult to weigh the sparrow and what he eats, but you could weigh the hamster and how much he eats every day for a week.' At the end of the week, Linda and her friends announced, 'The hamster ate more than twice as much as his own weight'. Linda then added, 'Now I'm going to find out how much I eat in a week'.

'What does the weather man mean?' Shirley wanted to know one foggy morning. 'He said the visibility is down to 25 yards on the motorway and my Dad said "I'm not driving in that. I'll go by train today." What's visibility? Why can't Dad drive in it?'

'I can swim,' said Eddy proudly on returning from his summer holiday. 'I can hold my breath under water and fetch a coin off the bottom of the swimming pool. I can hold my breath for hours.' Sue remained unimpressed. 'Get away with you,' she admonished. 'You can't hold it for a minute. I'll get the Pinger Clock and we'll try it.' Under her vigilant eye, Eddy discovered what a long time sixty seconds can seem.

In each of these situations, children were challenged by a personal problem in which mathematics came to their aid. Often they needed the help of the adult in thinking out a solution, but it was their own problem they solved, not one set by the adult. The inclusion in school of domestic play facilities, baking, sewing, scientific observation and experimentation, is not only a means of satisfying the child's emotional needs and his urge to explore. These experiences are also rich in mathematical opportunity, and an operation such as cooking tarts, for instance, may contain far greater mathematical challenge than the work sheets of an arithmetic book.

Infant teachers today are fully aware of the child's need to work through the concrete situation in which he can manipulate real objects towards abstract ideas. Yet many of our teachers tend to underestimate the child's capacity for best mathematical understanding.

Some excellent work has been done by the Nuffield mathematics team and other projects. The inspiration of Edith Biggs has led to many heart-searching experiments in schools all over the country. Yet when we examine what is happening in the vast majority of classrooms, improvement in the quality of mathematical experience for young children is hard to find. Firms producing mathematical apparatus issue what teachers ask for, yet when we examine these aids we find much which causes grave concern. Scientifically structured apparatus such as Dienes, Stern, Cuisenaire and other material designed by mathematicians with a deep understanding of the principles involved, serve an excellent purpose and are not here under consideration. What does call for examination is the vast quantity of apparatus which focuses on helping the child to memorise the relationship between number symbols and groups of objects.

In a classroom which is typical of many, children were allowed to select from a range of commercially produced number activities. Some were fitting jig-saw pieces together to form numeral and picture group associations. Others were performing a similar operation using numerals and groups of dots, while others were fitting pegs into holes on large wooden numeral shapes.

Some of these children knew the name of each numeral, yet when shown a small group of objects, they had little idea of how many there were in the group, or they started to count. One boy could recognise the correct number when shown a group of dots or pegs, but was uncertain when confronted with a group of assorted real objects. When asked to write the number 3, one girl drew an outline of the numeral and covered it liberally with dots.

In another part of the room, children were adding numbers together, and two of these children drew the appropriate number of dots and counted them in order to find the answer. One boy reached his conclusions by drawing imaginary dots in the air.

What impression will such exercises leave on the child's mind? His ability to obtain correct answers in this way may mask his lack of understanding. In later years, when he is required to deal with mathematical problems, which can only be solved if he knows what he's doing, these insecure foundations will be revealed. It is scarcely surprising that so many adults find mathematics a nightmare instead of the fascinating adventure it should be.

In another school, children were using work-books in which they were required to draw lines connecting symbols, or fill in outline shapes. Once the child had the hang of what he was expected to do, it was possible to complete the work-sheets with little or no understanding of the ideas each sheet set out to convey. Moreover, these work-books were expensive, and the children were expected to complete the exercise on tracing paper in order to preserve what was supposed to be expendable.

Number games are published and purchased in thousands. Most of them depend on the idea of throwing a dice, counting on or counting back, missing a turn, etc. There are many variations on the same theme, and in the course of the game, a child may need to recognise number bonds or make small calculations. While such exercises are pleasurable and harmless, by comparison with some of the interesting things the child could be doing, these are very meagre mathematical diet. The child may as a result memorise the symbols used and some of the number relations, but how far does such material deepen his understanding of the nature of numbers?

Many teachers feel obliged to produce some visible expression of number ideas which have had little opportunity to develop. As a concession to 'The New Maths', a gallery of pictograms and graphs paper their classroom walls, and superficial work on sets and graphs is frequently the only outcome of attempts to improve the mathematical education of young children.

Infant teachers are well aware that there is more to 'Infant Mathematics' than number symbols, elementary calculation and learning the measures, yet seem unable to use some of the child's basic problems which puzzle and fascinate, which have already stirred his mind and challenged his intellectual interest. There is nothing new about the mathematics available to the child's understanding. The approach may be new, but the aim as ever is to help the child to use mathematics as a means of simplifying the problems he meets in daily life with a view to solving them. Perhaps if we locked apparatus and work-books away in the cupboard for a while and allowed ourselves to become fully involved in the child's own absorbing interests, the way to mathematics would become clearer and the quality of the child's mathematical experience would improve.

Existing provision for mathematical experience in infant classrooms falls broadly into four categories. Few teachers limit experience to the manipulation of numbers on paper, but there are still some who offer little more than a jazzed-up version of traditional sums. The influence of recent attempts to improve the quality of mathematical education has produced two kinds of results. Some teachers use material and equipment as a means of instructional teaching of mathematical ideas, while others design carefully structured situations in which children are encouraged to 'discover' these ideas for themselves. In the fourth category we have those teachers who feel confident in helping children to develop understanding of the mathematics inherent in every experience of daily life. By far the greater number of teachers devote much of the children's time to what amounts to little more than jazzed-up sums, and the following classroom situation is typical of many.

Number and reading are associated in this school, mainly through the use of work-cards and number books. The children work in groups and their material is designed to cover three stages. Children working at stage one are using small trays, each of which bears a numeral. They have a good assortment of small plastic objects such as animals and cars. Dots alongside each numeral enable the child to contribute the appropriate number of plastic toys to each tray. Children at stage two are using a number line. They use pictorial work-cards as an aid to addition by counting on along the number line. When they reach stage three, similar simple addition is guided by work-cards on which the sum is spelled out in words and underneath the words, in numerals. At each stage, there are additional activities along similar lines. The sole aim of these activities is to enable the child to write down simple addition sums and obtain the correct answer, and by the end of the year the more able children graduate to writing 'number stories' in individual books. The teacher talks to the child who is unable to perform these tasks, but the child who gets his answers right on paper may have little discussion with her.

Mathematical experience in the following classroom is varied and sound, but still the demands made on the child are comparatively slight.

Again the children work in groups and all are involved at the same time in 'Mathematical Activities'. The emphasis is on measurement and the work is graded. In the first stages the children need to determine differences, for example, 'heavy and light', 'fast and slow', 'long and short', through handling objects and materials. They proceed to finer differences such as 'Heavier than but not so heavy as', 'Long, medium, short', etc. They record their findings verbally at first, and are later helped to record their observations in individual books, using pictures, words and numbers according to the ability of the child. In the next stage, each child is asked to estimate and then check the weight, height and length of prescribed objects. When he has some knowledge of the various units of measurement, he is given problem cards of which the following are typical.

'Go to the shops. Buy a loaf of bread and a pint of milk. How much change is there from 20p?'

'Find the tallest boy in the school.'

'Fetch a pint bottle and fill it with water. How much does the water weigh?'

Young children thinking

Materials in this room are plentiful and well designed, and the problems are in themselves interesting; although they are scarcely personal, they motivate sufficiently to make the work meaningful.

We will now follow Mrs B through the early part of one morning in a rather different type of classroom. The children enter the classroom in twos and threes and either carry on with a job from the previous day, or take up a fresh one. Susan and Kingsley wanted to paint. 'These pieces of paper are too big,' they complain to Mrs B. 'We're making little pictures today for the playhouse and we want them this size. These pieces will make four.' Mrs B showed them how to fold and cut the large sheet of paper. 'Now you have four pieces of equal size,' she explained. 'Each small piece is a quarter of the big sheet.' 'Quarter means four the same,' Kingsley informed Susan as they started to paint.

Glyn and Robert brought a collection of miniature cars. 'We need a garage,' said Robert. 'We want to make it in wood.' Mrs B nodded. 'You may use a piece of the best wood,' she said, 'but you can only have a piece this size and you must make a plan of the parts so that you don't waste any. You could cut out the parts in paper and fit them on to the wood before you begin to saw it up.'

'David and Dawn and me's making buns today,' said Wendy. 'I cut the recipe from Mum's mag. It says two parts flour, one part butter, one part sugar. . . . What's parts?' Mrs B explained the idea of proportion, and because the children needed to use the idea, it was understood.

Time after time during the day, Mrs B seized an opportunity as it arose, and these children were using mathematical skill as they acquired it, in fully meaningful situations. Periodically, perhaps once each week, Mrs B also engineered a situation which was structured either to introduce a number idea, or to extend and strengthen one the children had already discovered. The following are examples. She had a small collection of coins from different countries she had visited and she helped the children to devise games of exchange with them. Another time she assembled many different instruments used in measuring weight, and the children were asked to decide why so many different kinds were needed.

When our children become adults what will they need? A store of mathematical facts and the mere ability to compute, or the willingness to use their mental equipment to solve personal problems, together with a sense of pleasure in understanding and handling mathematical laws and ideas?

The choice is ours. We can aim either to cultivate prescribed and limited social skills, or we can encourage the growth of mathematical understanding and help the child to find lasting pleasure in those activities of the mind which impose an ordered pattern on every aspect of daily life.

8

The challenge of primitive materials

One way in which Primary teachers in the United Kingdom excel is in their selection and provision of creative materials. Usually these materials are varied and maintained in good condition, and children are encouraged to experiment freely in their chosen medium. Very few teachers expect the child to wait to be told what he can use and how he is to use it. They may intervene from time to time and guide the child by suggesting more effective techniques, but they rarely dominate. The child is allowed to develop a creative relationship with such rewarding materials as sand, water, wood, clay, paint and interesting waste materials. Indeed, it is in this aspect of learning that the most positive educational developments have taken place in recent years. It was through the free creative use of materials that classroom procedures first moved towards a liberal approach to education, and very few teachers choose to ignore these benefits to the child.

When teachers are asked why they include these materials and what they think children gain from using them, they usually express opinions such as, 'Children enjoy being creative. They need an outlet for the way they feel. I watch Johnny taking it out of the clay and I know he's getting rid of feelings which trouble him. Or Mary, here, had an exciting time discovering shells on the beach and she wants to prolong her pleasure and tries to model or paint, using the impressions left by the experience.' The replies of most teachers would follow similar lines and the emphasis is on the expressive use of materials as a means of enabling the child to develop emotionally, or communicate his creative ideas.

While this interpretation is good, it is incomplete. Rarely is the intellectual challenge of primitive materials taken into account, and what the child can learn from the materials themselves is too often ignored. What they have to teach him is as important as what he can do with them.

In handling simple basic materials the child is in much the same position as primitive man when he was faced with the unyielding rock, the elusive qualities of soil, the beneficial and yet terrible challenge of water, the rigidity and resistance of wood, or the pliable yet brittle qualities of clay. From these materials he had to fashion the things his mind designed. If he were to emerge from the cave, he must be able to exercise some control over the elements, and in order to gain mastery over them he was forced to learn about their behaviour and come to terms with what he discovered.

Man reared himself on two of his four feet, thus releasing two of his feet to become hands. He extended the use of his hands by devising tools. Later, he extended the use of his eyes, his ears, and his sense of touch with aids, which gave him still greater control. In other words, it was through meeting the challenge of primitive materials that man became intelligent and ultimately achieved supreme status in the world of living things.

The child and primitive man have much in common. Like early man, the child is confronted by materials which are as yet unexplored by him. What may be known about them by the adult has yet to be discovered by the young child, and he makes his discoveries through personal contact, not by being shown or told. Primitive materials present the child with the problems they provided for primitive man, and what made man intelligent is available in the materials for the child.

Left to their own devices, children respond readily to this challenge. They find infinite appeal in soil and mud, in sand and water, in making colourful marks on paper; later they enjoy the discipline of wood, of stone and rock, of sound and light. It is the crust of the earth, in all its variations, which most attracts the child. In handling these things the child's powers of concentration are exercised to the full. He is completely absorbed and happy because his deepest needs are satisfied.

Children all over the world behave in similar ways. Toddlers spend most of their lives near the ground, and what lies on top of it is the most obvious and natural plaything. Wherever the child finds soil and mud he has all he needs to keep him occupied, and the young of every nationality play with soil in similar ways. They scrabble in it, mould it into shapes and miniature landscapes, make mud pies, pile it to dam back a trickle of water and try the taste of it from time to time.

Soil and what it contains offers infinite variety. It is the stuff in which things grow. It contains sand, or chalk, or salt, or clay. It harbours pebbles and stones and rocks and crystals. Each of these materials has much to teach the child. Yet it is comparatively rare, for instance, to find soil in a classroom except when it is used for growing things. Sand is usually there, but how often is adequate provision made for discovering its properties and behaviour? Too often only wet sand is allowed because dry sand makes a mess on the floor. Salt is sometimes used, perhaps as a material which can be carved and chalk merely as writing medium, while substances such as cement, plaster of Paris, or fire-clay, are rarely found at all. Most classrooms provide clay, but usually it is used exclusively for modelling. Rocks and stones and fossils may appear on an investigation table, but comparatively little is done about helping the child to explore their nature. What usually happens is that the child collects information about them from books. Indeed, it is hard to find a teacher who is fully aware of the learning opportunities offered by these and other such fascinating materials, and without adult guidance, much in the way of discovery is lost to the child.

One teacher rediscovered the pleasure of soil when she moved into a new house and was confronted with the job of creating a garden. Her first, somewhat reluctant efforts, gained impetus and suddenly she began to feel like the Creator Himself as she struggled with soil and rocks and sand and clay to shape the ideas she had in mind. The highly educative nature of her materials was impressed on her and she decided to share her interest with the children. 'You can each bring a bag of soil from your own garden,' she told the children. 'And when you dig it up, try to find how deep the soil is and what lies underneath.'

The children were surprised when they saw the different soils side by side. The teacher added to the variety by contributing samples from the gardens of friends and relatives in more distant parts of the country. The specimens ranged from rich red loam, to yellow sandy soil and heavy dark clay and peat. 'We could make soil pictures with the different colours,' the children said. They were also amazed by the thinness of this crust on which all life depends. According to the measurements made by the children, it varied from as little as a few inches to several feet.

Samples of the soil were shaken up in water in glass jars and allowed to settle. Experiments with growing seeds in different soils and in each of the main components of soil were set up. Equal measures of different soils were weighed and compared. Tests were made to see which soils absorbed water rapidly, which dried out quickly, etc. The children began to understand why 'some plants grow better in some gardens than in others'.

They then turned their attention to sand. It was no longer

merely something they played with. It was part of the earth itself, and it became a source of intense interest. Their teacher brought them a good magnifying lens and the children examined different kinds of sand. The beauty of individual grains filled them with pleasure. They were interested in the way very fine sand clung to the skin like powder, and the amount of water which made different kinds of sand 'just right' for moulding. They wanted to know where the 'little pieces of rock' came from, and their teacher helped them to make sand by shaking stones together in water.

They poured sand of different textures through a funnel and noticed the way in which the resulting cone varied according to the nature of the sand. They made slopes of different sands and ran miniature cars down them to see 'which sand held the cars up' and which allowed the cars to run more freely down. They weighed equal measures of different sands and then set them out in 'order of heaviness'.

They then looked at chalk and salt and tried similar experiments with these materials. They compared the various results and found that some substances had unique qualities; for instance, salt dissolves in water, sand always falls apart when it dries out where clay goes hard, 'like rock', chalk powders easily, and so on.

It took a heavy fall of snow to replace this interest with another. The teacher looked round the room. With the various experiments cleared away, there was little to show. She had not insisted on written recording. Indeed, the experiments followed one another with such speed and enthusiasm, that there really was no time to write things down. The results of the work lay in the impressions retained by the children and a remark from one of the fathers was perhaps reward enough. 'I'm fixing a greenhouse,' he told her. 'Our Spencer here appears to be an authority on soils. He says he's just "done soil at school". He really knows more about it than I found in my gardening book.'

Watching children at play on a holiday beach provides many clues as to what can be learned from simple materials such as sand and rocks and water. One group of children, whose ages ranged from four to eight or nine, first made the traditional sand-castle with its moat which the sea was persuaded to fill. They then became more ambitious. 'We can use these big pebbles and bits of rock for a castle,' they suggested. 'We'll make it big enough to get inside. Shells will do for the floor like tiles. And the seaweed'll make lovely curtains.'

Not satisfied with pebbles, they selected boulders and rocks. One boy observed, 'You'll have to dig the sand away before you can move that one.' They worked hard to free the rock. 'It's too heavy,' they then decided. Now the rock was free it was difficult to move. 'We can't lift it. It needs a sledge thing to pull it along.'

They found pieces of driftwood and bound them together with stout string. They tied skipping ropes to their 'runners' and dragged the rock on to the sledge. They were then able to haul it into position.

'The pieces have to fit together,' one of the older boys suggested. 'I've watched the men at home building a stone wall and they make the pieces fit into one another.'

They also discovered that a sea wall with holes through which water could flow in and out withstood the battering of the waves, where a more solid wall would be washed away.

When constructing the outer walls of their castle, they began to realise the significance of the right angle. 'All the corners must be the same or the walls won't meet,' they decided.

Fitting shells into a pavement pattern was a fascinating occupation for the younger children. Sometimes their attention was diverted by speculation as to what had lived inside them and why there were so many different shapes; why some were thick and others thin; why some were smooth and others spikey, etc.

The fact that by the time they were called by their parents, the stone castle was scarcely more than a ground plan didn't reduce their enthusiasm. 'We'll carry on with it tomorrow,' they promised one another. 'It's smashing.'

The onlooker might well wonder whether these children had learned more during a day in the holiday than they did in a week at school.

Where children are free to learn from the elements and from the challenge of the earth in its natural state, there is no doubt at all about the quality of their learning. The child in the mountain village may be slow to acquire the social skills, but he is master of his own environment by the time he is eight or nine. The fisherman's son knows the laws of the sea. The farmer's son knows the laws of the land. Such knowledge is part of the child himself and of his way of life; it is not a set of facts he must retain in order to recall and have tested.

Noel first met clay when he was three and went to play-school. He tried unsuccessfully to do with it what he saw others doing. Noel was small for his age and by no means muscular. He soon discovered that clay was heavy material and that it needed quite strong muscles to control it. But he liked the feel of it when he smoothed the lump with wet fingers and he liked the way he could make marks in it. He experimented, using a comb, a nail, a fork and the handle of a spoon. The clay retained the impressions even when it dried out.

It wasn't until he was five and in the Infant School, that Noel really began to enjoy modelling with clay. He was given a huge lump and, now his hands were larger and stronger, he could hold it. It invited his fingers to slip round it. He could roll it round and round like a ball. He could roll it out longer and longer like a snake. He could squeeze it into interesting shapes. He tried making shapes by putting bits of it together, but this wasn't very successful and he learned to pull the shapes out from the solid lump instead.

When the clay was wet it was grey, but when it dried it became nearly white. If you put it near the radiator to dry it cracked and bits broke off. It had to dry slowly. When the new clay came it was a pretty reddish brown; Miss K said this was the clay which made plant pots and chimney pots, and she would take Noel and the others to show them where it all came from.

They visited the quarry and Noel had never seen so much clay. It was all in the ground and you didn't have to dig far to find it. Miss K said it was once hard rock called granite, but now it had gone rotten. They brought back a huge lump from the quarry and Miss K showed them how to knead it and cut it across with a wire and knead it again to press out all the air.

At home Noel's father was making a patio. 'It's a good use for this part of the garden,' he said. 'There's nothing but clay under here.' Noel helped to prepare the place for the patio and there sure enough was masses of smooth wet clay which wouldn't give way to his spade. This clay was blue with streaks of yellow, and it was really quite pretty. Father gave Noel a lump to play with, but it wasn't as nice as the clay at school.

One day after a holiday, the clay at school was dry and hard. Noel tried putting water on it, but that only made the lumps slimey. Miss K gave him a hammer and said, 'Hammer the lumps into powder. We'll have to make it up again.' Noel hammered the lumps until they cracked. He went on hammering until there was only powder and no lumps left. 'You can fill this can with water,' Miss K told him, 'and pour it over the powder. Then we'll cover it with a wet sack and tomorrow it will be ready to use.'

Noel was six when he went with his parents to stay in the Cotswolds. They visited a pottery and Noel was surprised to see grown men playing with clay. 'They make dishes out of all this clay just like I do,' he observed. 'It would be nice to have that spinning thing. I should like to have a go on that.'

77

The potter showed Noel how to press the lever which started the wheel and Noel watched the lump shape up and out beneath his hands. When they went outside he saw the big bins and he knew what they were. He explained to his father how the clay was made up, and the potter showed him the machine which kneaded the clay and pressed out the air. He saw the pots going into the big ovens and some coming out. He asked what 'glazed' meant and the potter showed him how the dishes were first painted and then glazed.

When Noel told Miss K about the visit she gave him a book about making pots and Noel was fascinated by the story of how people made pots in far-away places and in ancient times. He stared at the picture of a man from long ago who was making a bowl. 'I bet his bowl broke up like mine did,' he murmured, 'if he left it to dry in the hot sun.'

'We will visit the museum,' Miss K promised. 'There we can see pieces of pottery from ancient Rome and Egypt. I'll show you where the places are on the map when we come back.'

Noel's interest in clay and his experience of it gave him a personal link with the past and with people in foreign places. He had a deep and intimate knowledge of the material, of its nature and origin, and of the problems involved in mastering it. His knowledge of the material and the satisfaction he gained from handling and controlling it, provided him with an interest which seemed likely to be sustained throughout his life.

Noel learned a lot about clay because his teacher's own knowledge of it was good. She also knew when to intervene to give information, or add something to the situation which would carry the interest on. She planned progression in the child's handling of the material, and as his relationship with it matured, she made certain that it continued to challenge his mind as well as satisfy his emotional needs.

In Miss K's classroom, sand was another source of investigation. She had separate trays for dry and wet sand, and when the weather was good, the children had access to an outside sandpit. At the beginning of the year, the equipment Miss K put in the sand trays was simple. Scoops, containers of various shapes and sizes, a sieve, a rake and a funnel. The children learned much about the characteristics and behaviour of sand from this equipment; then other equipment was added a little at a time, such as a spring balance and scales, measures, a calibrated glass jar, moulds and cutters of various shapes, sandpaper of different grades and a strong magnifying glass.

There was much more scope in the sandpit outside. Nearby was a garden tap and Miss K provided a length of hose, some pieces of drain-pipe, a besom and a broom, large buckets and ropes. She also persuaded her boyfriend to screw a pulley to the overhanging eaves which ran alongside the sandpit. By the time her children were six, they knew almost as much about sand as the contractor in charge of motorway construction.

Other materials in Miss K's classroom received similar attention from time to time, so that at some point during the year, the children were encouraged to explore the nature of paint or colour, of paste and adhesives, of wood and water, as well as of less familiar materials such as putty, plaster of Paris, concrete and fire-clay.

Not only were the children intellectually interested, the effect of their understanding of the materials they used was reflected in the quality of their creative and expressive work. In this way, one teacher made maximum use of materials which are vital to man's development and in so doing, increased a hundred-fold the children's appreciation and delight in the world of materials in which they lived and were later to work.

9

The use of topics and themes

In recent years, the discovery approach to learning has been vigorously acclaimed. Teachers interpret this approach in different ways, using such terms as topic, theme, centre of interest, starters, etc., to denote a form of stimulation which encourages the child to 'find out for himself'. Enquiry may arise from the child's spontaneous interest, or it may be stimulated by material introduced by the teacher with a specified purpose in view. In work of this kind, children may share a common experience, but what each child takes from it is unique, and children are encouraged to learn as individuals.

Quite often the materials used to stimulate enquiry challenge thoughtful observation, but sometimes they do not and what little effort they demand may be misdirected. One or two examples will serve to illustrate the very variable quality of learning which has come to be labelled 'discovery'.

Attractive reference books lined the corridor of a Primary School. A boy of seven drifted along the corridor peering from jacket to jacket. When asked what he was doing he replied, 'I'm looking for my interest'.

He selected a book on prehistoric monsters and took it back to his classroom. There he spent the rest of the afternoon copying passages from the book into his 'interest book'. He obtained the help of a friend when it came to drawing pictures of some of the monsters. He spent each afternoon on his book and it was put amongst others in the reading corner on Friday. It looked neat and knowledgeable and the gold star on the cover acknowledged his labour.

Situations of this kind are by no means uncommon. At best a child tries to extract information from the text, perhaps with the help of his teacher, and then to reproduce it in his own words. The teacher may even supplement the contents of the reference book by supplying pamphlets, charts and diagrams, or pictures published by a newspaper firm. This may be a rather arid exercise in comprehension, but it isn't topic work. The child learns little from the way he works, and if he acquires information in the process his concepts will be flimsy and unrealistic.

In another school we find what at first glance appears to be excellent. The children are working individually, or in small groups. The range of their activities is extensive and each is related in a different way to the material used for investigation. These children are studying the way in which objects can be moved over a surface. One group is pushing a tin box about on the floor, trying it in different positions, with and without the aid of pencils used as rollers. Another group has a similar box to which they are attaching wheels. A third group is experimenting with the use of marbles and a few children are trying the exercise on different surfaces. All groups are actively involved and making illustrated records of their observations.

Closer investigation reveals the fact that each group is following the instructions on a card. Questioned about their experiments, one group explained. 'We're pushing the tin along the floor, and the pencils make it easier.' Another group replies, 'If you polish the floor the tin slides'. One child in this group adds, 'I slipped down on the floor in the hall last week'. The group with the wheels are carried away; 'It needs an axle thing. I made a lorry in Miss R's class and put the wheels on it with a nail and they fell off.'

This situation is a vast improvement on the former. Even so, further discussion with the children reveals the fact that the topic has been introduced by the teacher and entirely devised by her. The children are following instructions which correspond to lines of enquiry planned by the teacher. The topic exists in the mind of the teacher, and although these children are discovering things for themselves, the whole exercise lacks unity because the children are unaware of their terms of reference and unable to relate their discoveries to a central theme. They know what they are doing, but not why they are doing it.

This topic, in fact, originated in the mind of an author who writes articles for teachers and the stimulus came from an illustrated text in an educational journal. Many articles of this kind are excellent if used as a means of stimulating ideas on the part of the teacher, or as a source of information and guidance, but how they can be directly applied to situations unknown to the author is highly debatable. The teacher must first relate the idea promoted by the author to the situation in her own classroom. The material should be used by her, not merely transferred to the children.

It was the middle of March, and six-year-old children were screwing up scraps of pink tissue-paper and pasting them inside the outline of a tree. 'It's almond blossom,' they explained. 'It's for Miss D's frieze.' Other groups of children were applying wodges of cotton-wool, scraps of fabric or paint to outlines of lambs, flower heads and background scenery. They liked their teacher and were quite prepared to offer their services if it would please her. Miss D was happily arranging a display of 'yellow things' in one corner. Objects selected because they were different shades of yellow, were artistically arranged against a swathe of pale green crepe. The classroom looked gay and attractive and everyone was happy except an intelligent little girl who grew somewhat impatient with her pink tissue-paper screws and slipped away behind a screen into the book corner where she rapidly became absorbed in a book.

Miss D described her topic as Spring. 'I've talked to the children about lambs,' she said. 'And I've read them some poems about daffodils and primroses. There's an almond tree in full bloom at the corner of the school playground. All the work is related to the child's immediate experience.'

Miss D was thoroughly sincere. She had read and acquired the right words, she had the co-operation of the children, but what were they learning? How far had the work stemmed from their impressions of their immediate environment? Had they really observed the almond tree? And if they had, was filling in the teacher's outline with pink tissue-paper screws really their own impression of such observation?

Miss D's guiding aim was to produce a spectacular effect. She also wanted to 'keep the children happy', but is this education? Unwittingly she was sacrificing their opportunity to learn, for the sake of something to show. Such ideas as existed were hers, and any ideas gained by the children were pale images of her ideas.

Experience and study have stocked the mind of an adult with ideas. A teacher may have brilliant ideas on behalf of her children. But children have ideas of their own, and if the teacher will not acknowledge this, their ideas may wilt unnourished. A responsibility of the teacher is to let children have ideas of their own. If she insists on trying to put her ideas into the minds of children, their minds will be clogged with sterile, inert material and the opportunity to learn and think for themselves will be lost to them.

Miss D could initiate a Spring theme by helping the children to use their almond tree as a starting point. Aesthetic reactions to its beauty may colour their approach. Improved observation can expand rather than diminish their pleasure, and when the petals begin to fade and drop, consternation about this ephemeral state of affairs may provoke further enquiry. When

83

the children have assimilated what they can from this experience, they may feel urged to communicate some part of it. If Miss D is wise she will provide a suitable range of materials with which the children can translate their impressions into some tangible form, but she must not expect a spectacular frieze to decorate her classroom walls.

Too often the process of 'finding out for oneself' is interpreted by the teacher as finding out from books, or from the teacher with perhaps the help of visual aids. There is certainly a place for finding out from the words of other people, but in the early stages children learn most actively through direct contact. They obtain information through their eyes, their ears and the sense of smell or taste and most vitally of all through the skin. Any child will learn more in a few minutes about a coconut by handling one, than he will learn in an hour by reading a book about coconuts, or from listening to a lengthy account of them from his teacher.

Discovery starts with real objects put into the hands of children, or with personal experience in a live situation. Even far-away places and events can be associated with the child's personal life. The teacher may be unable to bring the African warrior to dance for the child, but she can let the child handle an African drum, or create his own version of a tribal dance.

Investigation starts in the thoughts of the child as he handles materials, and the quality of his thinking depends on the quality of his materials. Imagination is the faculty of forming images in the mind, and good images are the raw material of imagination. Thoughts will not develop, imagination will not function, unless the child has formed impressions, and realistic impressions are the result of first-hand experience, not of being told.

Anything other than solid, three-dimensional material is merely an aid, or substitute for first-hand experience. The most satisfying substitute for the real thing is perhaps a film, which gives an impression of three dimensions and of movement. Photographs suggest three dimensions but have no action. Pictures are poor substitutes for photographs or films. Drawings and diagrams are highly symbolic, and although these aids can be used when it is impossible to use the real thing, we should have no illusions as to their effectiveness. How much, for instance, can a child learn about a cow from a two-dimensional paper picture the size of a textbook? Sometimes we can focus attention on some aspect of an object by showing a picture, or perhaps a painting, or extend first-hand observation by the use of a film, but we should remain perfectly clear about the part these aids play, and preparing for topic work doesn't mean merely ordering a film or collecting pictures.

What does a child learn, for instance, from a picture of a post-office? How does it compare with what he finds in the post-office round the corner? What thoughts are stirred by plastic cocoa-pods and dummy packets of chocolate? Why use such substitutes if the real thing is available?

Sometimes teachers turn to educational periodicals where suggestions for investigation and study topics appear regularly. These features can serve as a means of sparking off an idea, but they are rarely intended to be used as they stand and to present them straight from the page is unimaginative and can lead to work which bears little relationship to what children need.

The best use a teacher can make of such material is to examine the principles embodied in the topic and then relate these principles to her own teaching situation. The author's material, objectives and methods of presentation may be excellent, and, wisely used, can be of great help to inexperienced teachers. But the reader must take the trouble to interpret such suggestions in the light of what she knows about her pupils and in relationship to their experience as individuals.

A feature on traction engines, for instance, appeared in one periodical. Some fascinating photographs of machines in use during the early part of the century were accompanied by information about the engines themselves and about the use made of them by farmers since the middle of the nineteenth century.

One teacher, who was in the habit of using this weekly feature and who in fact bought the periodical for that purpose, cut out the pictures and mounted them to form a frieze. She talked to her seven-year-old children about the pictures, giving them little opportunity to ask questions, or to voice their own experience. She then composed a sentence about each picture and wrote these at the foot of the frieze. The children were then told to draw the engines and write up the sentences in their topic books. These children lived in a town and they were fascinated by the engines. Many of them had visited a local engine museum, or had seen engines being used by fair people. They had a considerable amount of experience which could have been shared and extended, but the teacher never gave them a chance. She believed she had taught them something, when, in fact, they had much they could have taught her.

Another teacher who purchased the same periodical, kept such features by for use when the occasion arose. Some weeks later, this teacher initiated an interest in 'What Makes Things Work?', starting with a collection of mechanical toys, old clocks, and domestic appliances. One child brought the model steam engine he'd received as a Christmas present. He lit the methylated-spirit stove and demonstrated the way in which the steam drove the pistons. Steam-driven motors caught the imagination of one group of boys and experiments in making their own steam turbines, from a treacle tin filled with water and a wheel made from a milk bottle top, kept them absorbed for two or three days. The teacher then remembered her photographs and used them to extend discussion. She drew from the children their individual impressions and experiences of steam-driven engines and set them to work to find out how much fuel and water these engines needed to keep them going.

The boys readily recognised the reasons for changing over to petrol engines and began to compare modern and out-dated engines. Some of them looked ahead and tried to forecast the engines of the future in the year 2000. It was at this point that some of the boys tried to reproduce pictures of the engines in the photographs and place them alongside fantastic designs of their own, adding a few notes of explanation beneath their drawings.

Where the youngest children are concerned the teacher has an overwhelming advantage. Children entering school are meeting materials and events as for the first time. They grow daily more aware of their surroundings, and although objects surround the child from birth, many are not noticed until the child reaches a certain stage in his cognitive development. The freshness of first discovery enhances the most humble object, and for children of five and six, the environment teems with unexplored delights.

Some interests start from collections made by the children themselves. The teacher may spark off an idea and then encourage the children to search for suitable material. Natural objects, things which are old, things that work, shiny things, wheels and balls, are interests that lend themselves to this approach.

Helping to unpack the school stock gave rise to an interest in paper. The teacher suggested that the children should find as many kinds of paper as possible. The collection ranged from newspaper and tissue-paper to finely woven notepaper and reinforced wrapping paper. The teacher contributed a selection of hand-made papers. Later she added parchment and helped the children to make 'papyrus' from reeds.

Some topics develop through the teacher's skill in detecting an embryonic interest. A boy of six fell in the playground and grazed his knee. A few days later his teacher noticed him picking at the scab. 'I shouldn't do that, Tony,' she said. 'You'll make it bleed again. If you wait a bit longer the scab will drop off by itself.'

Tony scowled but desisted. Later in the day he came back to his teacher. 'Look at it now,' he said. 'I've got it off and it's skin underneath. How did it get some new skin?' His friends gathered round waiting for the teacher's reply. She showed them minor scars of her own and explained as simply as possible how skin repairs itself. This led to further questions about 'how the skin keeps everything else inside'. The outcome of this incident was an intense interest in the child's own body which persisted for several weeks.

On another occasion, a child of seven acquired a model typewriter for Christmas. She brought it to school with ambitious plans for 'writing a long book like those in the book shop'. A boy in the same class received an airmail letter and wanted to know why 'Par Avion' was printed beneath 'By Air Mail', and whether the letter came all the way in an aeroplane. A slightly older boy spent Sunday afternoon walking the moors with his parents. On Monday he brought the skeleton of a sheep's head to school and told his friends it was 'pre-historic'. Each of these incidents provided a starting point, and the teacher was able to develop interests which arose directly from the children.

Other interests are teacher-inspired. Miss B, for example, assembled an excellent collection of objects made from wood in the hope that she could interest the children in man's many uses of the material. She selected a wooden bowl, finely carved and polished to bring out the grain. She had always enjoyed this particular object because it was the work of a skilled craftsman and because she loved the material from which it was made. She was prepared to share her appreciation with the children and was not afraid of letting them see how she felt about it.

One child asked, 'Please can I feel it?' She had noticed the way in which Miss B fingered the polished surface and wished to share the experience. 'Did this wood really grow on a tree?' she asked.

Another child wanted to know, 'how the man made the bowl round', and a boy with a practical turn of mind asked, 'What's it for?' Another noticed, 'It's got different colours'. Miss B explained that there are many kinds of wood and promised to bring the children pieces of wood from different kinds of trees.

In this way the teacher stimulated the interest, and through discussion helped the children to identify several lines of investigation. She used their ideas as a guide to her selection and display of further materials, and the children's thoughts were already centring round studies, such as the origin and characteristics of wood as a creative medium, how the craftsman works and what he makes, and the many uses of wood in daily life.

In each of these situations, free discussion played an important part in opening up ideas in the child's mind. Each child needs to be actively involved and may need the encouragement and support of the teacher in making his contribution. Questions come naturally to the enquiring mind and spontaneous questions always indicate the beginning of thought and understanding. But these questions will not arise unless the material is thought-provoking and the mind of the teacher has a key role in every form of enquiry.

Sometimes the teacher's questions serve as a means of promoting observation and investigation. Skilful questions can open up profitable lines of enquiry. Paul, for instance, brought to school a toad he had found in the park. He put it in the aquarium 'to keep it wet'. His teacher rescued the toad and asked Paul, 'Where did you find the toad? Can you see his eyes? Tell me about them. Has he any eyelids? Can you see his ears, his nostrils? How does he breathe? How does he eat? How does he move on land; and in water? Tell me about his skin. Where does he live? Do you think he will be happy inside the water?'

Questions of this kind are open-ended. They improve observation and open up enquiry. They help to expand and deepen experience and suggest further lines of investigation.

Investigation may lead to an answer, or bring about the solution to a problem, but the most educative effect of investigation is experience, or the impressions received by the child in pursuit of his goal. Merely having experience may not however leave a lasting impression, and experience needs to be used in order to achieve its full educative effect. Using experience is a means of expressing reactions to it, and children should be offered a variety of modes of expression suited to their aptitudes and stage of development.

Impressions are readily translated into words by children who have a good vocabulary. Younger children will talk about their experiences if there is someone to talk to. Sometimes a young child will talk to himself. Talking out his impressions helps the child to clarify and extend them, and the quality of thought which experience leaves behind is vastly enriched through the use of words. Talking and writing are closely associated, particularly as the child becomes more confident in his ability to put words on paper.

Sometimes the simple description of the young child can develop into discussion with the teacher or with other children. A child of seven or so may be capable of giving a short talk to other children. The more able child may extend his written record into a systematic log. Books, letters, reports for classroom news sheets, perhaps accompanied by charts, diagrams and graphs are useful ways of recording experience.

Not all children find verbal recording easy and even those who do should be encouraged to use other modes of expressing experience and recording impressions. Drama and puppetry, model-making, picture-making and movement in the shape of dance provide helpful channels of communication for many children. Sometimes the children can extend material supplied by the teacher by making collections to illustrate some idea or conclusion.

Where the teacher succeeds in provoking thoughtful enquiry on the part of the child and then provides the means of translating the thoughts which stir in his mind, she has set the scene for educational growth and given him the best possible opportunity to participate in his own intellectual development.

The fundamental need is for the teacher to provide material which will provoke enquiry. The teacher knows in advance what the child *can* discover from investigation of the material, but this is not the same as deciding in advance what he *shall* discover. The questions come initially from the child, and a test of the provision made is the range and type of questions provoked by it. The teacher's questions are used to sharpen observation and to extend it. Answers to the teacher's questions can vary from child to child according to the nature of his individual investigation. In other words, each child's experience in any situation is unique, and observation is not a means of reaching the answer that is in the teacher's mind.

The teacher shares the experience with the child, but she doesn't attempt to make him have her experience, to see only what she sees and to reach a goal she has pre-determined. There is all the difference in the world between knowing what children can learn and deciding in advance precisely what they shall learn. The ultimate aim in work of this kind is to offer full scope for the child's natural curiosity, and to help him to develop habits of learning through enquiry which will provide him with a starting point in each new situation. We may not know the problems the child will meet as an adult, but we can equip him now to tackle them when they come.

In successful investigation, the teacher neither dominates nor abdicates; she participates, working with the child, sometimes taking the lead and sometimes letting the child lead her.

10

The child's view of the abstract world

The process of growing up involves the child in a state of constant conflict between his developing awareness of self and of his world of inner reality, and the demands made on his attention by the world of external reality. Life consists of reconciling these two realities, each dependent on the other and yet so often at variance.

We are all in the same position, but the child's point of view differs fundamentally from the view of the adult. Small children haven't lived long enough to know what is meant by the past or the future. The only time they know is now and, untrammelled by reviewing past events or planning for the future, they can focus their entire attention on what immediately affects them. The moment, with its internal or external experiences, is all.

The child's approach to his world is essentially bound up in his sense of curiosity and wonder and in his dawning understanding. In the early years, curiosity and wonder predominate. Understanding is a slow and evolutionary growth process. Because it is as yet only in the formative stages, the child is unaware that many problems of the universe are not soluble by man. To the young child all things are possible. His questions are radical and often metaphysical. Unaware of the enormity of his task, his mind seeks to grapple with the nature of infinity, of life and death, space, the rhythm of the universe and God.

I can remember as a child of five, lying on my back in a meadow gazing into the sky and asking myself, 'What is beyond?' My mind reached behind the clouds towards the deep blue firmament and began searching. 'But what is beyond that, and then beyond and beyond and beyond . . .?' until I became so overwhelmed by the immensity of it all I had to close my eyes and find reassurance within my inner world. I never talked to an adult about such an experience, and each time it occurred the question became more insistent.

During the first months of life, much of the child's world, apart from himself and his mother, is man-made. His first contact with the stuff of the earth is usually in the shape of water and air, and later soil. These primitive materials together with such natural phenomena as the weather, the rhythm of the seasons, volcanoes, earthquakes and the like, impinge upon him during his early years. By the time the child enters school, he has sufficient experience of them to give rise to questions, speculation and elementary reasoning.

Clive, watching his mother making pastry, said, 'I don't want a piece of dough today. I'd rather have some soil. Daddy's used up all the soil in the garden. Make me some more.' His mother's simple explanation of weathering and soil formation triggered off an unexplored avenue of mental activity. 'But how did the rocks come? Where did the wind start? If the rain stops it might not start again. . . .' This stream of thought culminated in the inexplicable. 'But if nobody made all that, who made it?' The answer, 'God', only increased the mystery.

Watching children at play with primitive materials, the adult becomes aware that a number of things may be happening. To begin with, curiosity dominates; experimentation may first of all result in discovery of what the material can do and what can be done with it. The material at this stage may serve as a medium, a vehicle of communication, a means of expressing emotions, or of provoking a creative outlet for impressions and reactions.

Very often the child's developing awareness of man's elementary materials is thought by the teacher to stay at this level, and creative work is usually the main reason for including these materials in the environment. The teacher may even be disappointed when the child ceases to produce some visible result of his manipulation. What may very well be happening is that awareness has reached the level of wanting to know not only what materials will do, but why they act in this way.

The why of the volatile nature of water, the clinging properties of granular material, the impregnable nature of stone, are now associated with wonder, which is something children have time for. The wonder of a rainbow is indeed a more enjoyable experience than its explanation, and the young child reserves the right to cling to the now which holds him in its spell.

Ultimately, personal experience, linked with the experience of others, brings understanding. Some of the magic is gone, and yet understanding leads on to further unexplored and wondrous worlds. Curiosity, wonder, understanding; this is the mental cycle of the young child, and the perceptive adult will link what she offers the child in the way of teaching and materials to what is happening in his mind. If the clay itself, or the colour in paint, now becomes a source of fresh investigation rather than a form of creative medium, then her teaching is linked to that.

New tins of paint arrived at one school, and were opened. The children admired the clear fresh colour of the unused powder. Early exploration of colour, e.g. 'All the blues we can make,' was revived. The teacher took up the theme of colour and provided material which enabled the children to consider colour significance, such as the role of green in nature, the blue of the sky, the colour of food and colour blending.

A fundamental need of the young child is movement. Movement of the body is accompanied by movement of the mind and imagination. Learning of any kind grows out of some form of movement, and where there is no movement, no growth is taking place. Observation of the young child makes the adult intensely aware of his need of and interest in movement. The baby may take little interest in an object until it starts to move and the action toy, either large like a scooter, or small like a top, remains in great favour throughout childhood.

By about the age of three the child becomes aware that some things move of their own accord and some things have to be activated through some form of extrinsic energy. The fusion of ideas about animate and inanimate objects persists into the Infant School, and even the boy of six who saw a helicopter for the first time wasn't sure. 'Is it a thing that does it by itself,' he asked, 'or has it got an engine?'

The child's curiosity about both forms of activation is intense. The six-year-old who pulled the wings off a fly wasn't cruel. He was asking the question, 'What makes it fly when it's so little? Has it got radar?' While we do not, of course, encourage investigation that causes injury to living things, we can encourage questions and try to help the child to satisfy his curiosity verbally. An investigation of moving things is a topic of vital interest at this stage.

From the point of view of the very young child, 'moving' and 'living' are synonymous. As he begins to understand the difference between energy of biological origin and energy harnessed or generated by man, his fascination grows. Investigation of levers, screws, pulleys and other simple mechanical principles shows him how energy can be maximised. Small girls as well as small boys want to find out how the watch, the car, or the kitchen gadget works. The same intense interest is extended to finding out what makes insects and animals move and this interest reaches its peak in the movement of the child's own body.

The child's own body, indeed, is a world of miraculous things to him and provides one of the richest sources of investigation the teacher can find in the classroom environment. One teacher made a short film of the children's hands and used this as a starting point for a study of 'How our hands and feet move'. She herself noticed much she had paid scant attention to before and was delighted by the variety and quality of the movement she observed.

The birth of a new member of the family is an event of intense interest experienced by many young children. Most teachers help children to adjust to this event and learn something from it. Many parents, indeed, turn to the school for assistance in satisfying the child's curiosity about birth, and unhealthy attitudes to procreation are virtually a thing of the past.

The child's intense and healthy interest in the phenomena of life also includes the phenomenon of death. 'Bang! Bang! You're dead', young Billy drops to the ground obligingly. 'And you'll stay dead for the rest of your life.' Billy makes an unnatural effort to remain still. When death occurs, movement is terminated and that's what death means to him at this stage.

'Sandy's died.' The loss of David's cat had a more profound effect on him than the death of his rather remote auntie. 'Dad's buried him in the garden.' Later on in the morning, David explained to a group of avid listeners, 'He'll stay dead in the ground and the worms will eat all his fur and his body. Then he won't be able to pounce out and kill the birds.' David is puzzled. His conception of death is embryonic, and death doesn't yet mean the total extinction of life.

The death of a person on whom the child depends may mean the unhappiness of separation, the deprivation of one who satisfies personal needs, or the withdrawal of a loved companion. The child may even feel guilty; 'Gran's gone away for

96

always. She got tired and poorly and she wants a rest. And it's not fair. I always go to see her on Sunday and now I can't. And if she'll come back, I won't break her best cup again.'

Children need to talk to understanding adults about these events. Their needs are intellectual as well as emotional, and the comforting assurance that, 'Grannie is happy where she is and even though she can't come back she is still thinking about you', isn't good enough. Adult fear of death, the attitude that children must be protected from knowing that death is an aspect of life and that its inevitability is all part of the wonderful cycle of existence, fosters unhealthy and disturbing attitudes in children. Indeed, an adult's fear of death can in part be attributed to such attitudes on the part of those who reared him. To the young child death is as interesting as life, and adequate understanding at each stage in mental development can help him to retain a balanced view and a sense of wonder rather than fear. Wonder and fear are very closely associated. As adults, whether we wonder or fear in the face of life's mysteries depends on the way our curious interest has been handled as children.

What we can help the child to understand is the idea of order, of the structure and pattern which supports the universe. The recurring rhythm of the seasons, the life and death cycle of plants, of butterflies, of the fish in the aquarium. The child has thought about these events, but he needs the help of the adult when formulating ideas and putting them into words.

The most fascinating part of the world, of course, is people and how they behave. The child's idea of himself as an individual is sufficiently well established to be used as a framework of reference. He is reaching out, often through dramatic play, towards an understanding of other people. He is anxious to find out what it feels like to be the doctor, his parents, the Queen, an astronaut or an Olympic gold medallist. Helping him to talk about these play experiences enables him to clarify and to extend his ideas. The drama of the classroom can be a starting

97

point for further enquiry which, in turn, will enrich his play. He should be encouraged to form and express an opinion about his own behaviour and about the way others behave, and when he has expressed his opinion it should be respected.

A child is observant, for instance, of adult attitudes to different people. 'You can't come in this way,' said Val, firmly closing the Wendy House door on the greengrocer. 'You have to go round to the back. Only visitors can come in at the front.'

George wanted a ride on the trolley. 'This is a bus,' he announced, 'and I'm an old grandpa. Now you'll have to give me a push.'

In another part of the room Alison swirled a mouldering fur cape round her shoulders. 'I'm a posh lady,' she informed her retinue. 'You have to bow, like to the Queen, and do what I want.'

A study of the views of Piaget and others on children's thinking has impressed on teachers the need for concrete experience in the early stages of conceptual development. Where young children are concerned, the concrete situation gives rise to thinking, but the thinking need not remain restricted to the concrete situation. It is precisely at this point that the child needs the help of the adult in making his first advances into the world of abstractions. His thoughts may remain associated with what he has assimilated from a concrete experience, but they are not bound by it. He is anxious to reach towards more complex thinking structures and this is precisely what adults must help him to do.

11

On becoming a person

There was a time when personality was thought to be inherited, and when people firmly believed that there was little to be done about the type of personality parents handed on to their off-spring. Scientific observation of personality development has modified this view. Today most adults are aware of the part played by learning and environmental influences in the shaping of a person. Personality is no longer regarded as unchangeable. While the basic personal pattern persists through life, it is always subject to modification, because it develops to a considerable extent through learning.

It is not our business in this chapter to consider the development and importance of personality. This is a vast and fascinating study beyond the scope of this work, and all we can seek to do here is to indicate the part played by mental activity on the part of the child during the process of becoming a person.

Although the personality pattern is not inherited, what the child brings with him at birth forms the basis of his person and influences the way events turn out. He can be said to inherit the hard core of his future personality. His physical body, his intellectual capacity with its mental characteristics and his predisposition or temperament, are his from birth for the rest of his life. Physical and intellectual possibilities and limitations are pre-determined and he will be predisposed to deal with life in a manner which characterises his temperament. How far his abilities and aptitudes develop and are used depends on the physical and social environment in which he is reared. The interaction between the hard core of him and what life brings to him will make him the person he ultimately becomes. He will, in short, learn how to be a person.

In the early days of life the child is conscious, but not conscious of himself. Gradually he learns that although he is a part of the world, he is a separate entity. This separate entity is unique and is recognised as such by others. He is a self and he differs from all other selves.

Once the child has formulated an idea of his separate self and then of what that self is, he can be said to be conscious of self. In formulating this idea of self he has been involved in simple forms of thinking. Thinking of an elementary kind develops, as do other aspects of the child, from birth. It is not, however, until the child is aware of himself that he can think about thinking and begin to think about himself.

The concept of self is a unified blend of thoughts and feelings. The self idea enables the child to become aware of who he is and what he is like.

It is difficult to imagine how a child would develop an idea of himself if it were not from other people. The way in which he deals with things and situations helps him to formulate his self idea and he does this by comparing his own behaviour with what he observes of the way others behave. How does he know that he is strong, for instance, until he discovers that he can lift a bucket of sand where another child needs to drag it along the shore?

The way other people treat him, what they say about him and to him, have a powerful influence over how he sees himself. What others expect of him, for example, acts as a guide to what they think he is capable of. In others the child sees his self as it were in a mirror. This gives rise to thoughts about himself and he learns to see himself as he thinks others think of him.

Self awareness is a dual concept. There is the physical self of flesh and bones, strengths and weaknesses, needs and interests, capabilities and failings; and there is a psychological self which exists purely in the mind. The child may learn to think of himself as kind, good, brave and generous, or as mean, bad, frightened and generally unlovable. Although this self exists only in the minds of himself and others, it exerts a constant and overwhelmingly powerful influence over the physical self. It is usually the psychological self that selects from available situations the one in which the child becomes involved. In other words, what happens to the child is the result of psychological selection, and what happens to him makes him what he is.

The development of personality is most rapid during the foundational years, and the critical period is from birth to the age of six or seven. During this period, under normal circumstances, parents and teachers are by far the most influential people in the life of the child. When they are aware of their role, there is much they can do to help the child to form the realistic view of himself which is essential to the development of an integrated person.

In some respects the relationships the child makes outside the home have a greater influence on personality development than those made within it. At home the child is an integral part of the family and is rarely seen objectively. He tends to see himself as part of the family rather than as a person in his own right. His relationship with his teacher is often the first opportunity the child has of gaining an objective idea of himself. His teacher sees him as an individual alongside other individual children, and not as an extension of herself. She also introduces him to wider cultural ideas of the kinds of people that together make an ethnic group. She shows him a wider choice of self images than the home can offer him.

Bearing these points in mind, we may now consider the gradual growth of the child's idea of himself.

To begin with, the baby's experiences are undifferentiated. He is wholly whatever he is feeling, cold, wet, hungry, or contented. He doesn't know he is any of these things, they are him and what he is. During the first months of life, he receives impressions and responds to them, but without the awareness of an intervening self. His learning consists of what Piaget calls 'sensory-motor' experiences, and from his point of view there are no boundaries between himself and his environment. What he holds in his hand is part of himself.

At six months, Jeremy enjoyed watching his own hands. With his fingers he explored the extent of his body. He put his foot in his mouth and cried with pain when he bit his own toe, but he was obviously not aware that he had hurt himself. At about the same time he waved his arms and legs gleefully when his mother spoke to him, but when a stranger appeared he lay still. He was beginning to be aware of differences between external objects.

By the time he was eight months, Jeremy could crawl. When he bumped against a chair he was annoyed and sometimes cried. Then one day he became angry and hit the chair with his fist. This was the first indication that he was aware of an object which existed outside of himself, that there was a personal self and other things which were not part of that self.

At the age of twelve months, Rebecca recognised her own dolly and when it was held out to her she said, 'Dolly!', but she was nearly sixteen months old before she clutched it hard and said, 'Mine!' A few months later, she would hold up her arms and say 'Becky up' (lift her up). She was nearly two before she used the pronoun 'I'.

By the time Rebecca was 2 years 6 months, the idea of 'mine' and 'yours' fascinated her, and everything she handled had to be identified as 'mine', or 'not mine'. She and her older brother were given similar sponge ducks by their auntie. When Rebecca clutched her duck and said 'Mine', Auntie responded, 'Yes. That's yours. That's Rebecca's duck.' Rebecca swiftly replied, 'It's not yours.' In a moment of insight she recognised the difference between the use of 'yours' in the two situations.

We begin to see the importance of language in helping the child to identify what is self and not self. From about the age of two, language plays an important role in the development of ideas about the self.

One of the first words a child learns is his own name, and once he is able to identify and label himself, he has formed a concept to which further ideas can be added. Mothers who talk to their children from the moment they meet them at birth, are helping them in many ways. Where the development of personality is concerned, attention of this kind helps to make a child feel singled out, a special individual. Mothers normally use the child's name as they talk. 'Nicholas has one little nose. Nicholas has two big eyes. Nicholas is going to have his bath' and so on. Nicholas is aware that mother's interest is directed towards him, and he soon learns to attach the sound of his name to himself.

Even before the age of two, Mother can encourage the child to think of himself in realistic terms and to accept himself as he is. She may want to think of him as completely dependent on her, but that idea of himself will be of little help to him. 'Yes. You can put on your own socks. There. Try again. Turn it this way round. That's right. You've done it. Now you can put them on by yourself every day.'

Encouraged in this way, the child will learn to think of himself as a separate and independent being, and much as Mother may want to keep him as part of her being, she expresses genuine love for her child when she acknowledges his separate existence. In later life, the child most loves and respects those who have helped him to think of himself as self-dependent.

In the early stages of the development of self ideas, the self image is not easy to hold, and in play the child easily loses his self identity. He becomes transformed into a train, or a dog, or some other person. His real self and the fantasy self readily fuse, and sometimes the fantasy self becomes a real and separate person, taking the mind form of an imaginary playmate.

Darren was four when 'Kelly' became his imaginary playmate. Darren had a baby sister in whom he was disappointed as a playmate, and there were no other children of his age in the neighbourhood. 'Kelly' was consulted on every occasion. He had a place at the table, a hollow for his head in the pillow and his own piece of soap in the bath. 'Kelly' was often the less favourable self, and when Darren was blamed for bouncing a ball into the geranium bed, it was 'Kelly', of course, who had made the mistake. The relationship between Darren and 'Kelly' was thoroughly healthy, and when Darren eventually entered school, 'Kelly' faded from the picture.

There is a noticeable correspondence between intelligence and imagination, and it is very often the highly intelligent child who creates a vivid and persistent imagined companion. He literally thinks into existence the playmate he wishes for himself. Occasionally the imaginary playmate is retained even when the child enters school and has adequate companionship. In rare cases the child becomes dominated by the imaginary playmate, and this state of affairs is usually indicative of emotional instability, probably of a temporary nature. Normally, however, the imaginary playmate marks a stage in personal development and is perfectly healthy and often a great pleasure to the child.

When the child enters school, the ideas he has formed about himself are dramatically extended. For one thing, he discovers a fresh need in himself, a need for the love of a significant adult outside the family circle. At this stage, the new love may take precedence over all others. The love of the adult inside the home is his by right, but the love of the adult outside the home is something he has to earn. His teacher's aims and standards may be very different from those with which he is familiar, but in order to secure her approval, he must develop a self which measures up to her idea of him. If she expects him to speak more carefully, to be a responsible person, to deal competently with tasks allocated to him, then he must accommodate.

He must also meet the challenge of many others like, and yet unlike, himself. He must belong to a group in which the rules of membership have already been established, and if the rules decree that boys play fair, share things and don't cry, then he must acquire these qualities as part of his personality. The psychological pressures on the child are very great, and many parents find their children exhausted at the end of those first days in school.

There are many ways in which a sensitive teacher can be of infinite help to the child. To begin with, the school situation in itself enables the child to discover himself as a person who belongs to a family but has a life which is apart from it. He may even enjoy keeping the events in this life secret from his parents. He brings with him into school the self which is a product of the way the family views him as an immature member. In school he discovers that there are other terms of reference. He is faced with many choices and he is free in his new-found independence to make up his mind for himself. What he ultimately becomes as a person will be the result of many personal decisions. In order to be independent he must learn to think and make decisions, and then to act upon his own decisions and accept the consequences.

While the school community faces him with decision-making opportunities, it provides him with experienced guidance on the part of the teacher. The skilful teacher will ensure, first of all, that the child meets the need to make decisions and then that he takes the responsibility of any decision he makes.

Modern practice in the Infant School classroom is based on choice on the part of the child. From a wide range of situations, the child is encouraged to select materials and jobs which are of specific interest and purpose to him. Under the vigilant observation of his teacher he decides his own job, and then the teacher stands by to see that he fulfils his responsibility to the chosen task.

Sara was interested in the gerbils. She had never experienced pets at home and now felt highly protective towards the small furry animals which depended on others. She asked for the daily job of feeding them and cleaning out their nest. She fulfilled her duties punctiliously for three days, then on Thursday in the heat of a fresh enthusiasm, she forgot. Sara's teacher remarked, 'Pip and Squeak look unhappy this morning. Have you fed them, Sara?' Sara shook her head. 'I'm doing clay,' she said. 'My hands are all covered in clay.' Her teacher persisted. 'Then you must wash your hands. You can leave your clay and no one will touch it while you feed your friends. You asked for the job this week and we all expect you to do it each day until we go home for Saturday and Sunday.' Sara grinned. 'They can't do it themselves,' she agreed. 'Anyway, it doesn't take a minute.'

Bill was much more difficult to deal with. He was intensely interested in scientific investigation and became particularly enthusiastic about simple devices for measuring time. He constructed a 'water-clock', a 'sand-timer', and calibrated a candle. He chattered knowledgeably about his experiments, but made no attempt to record in written form although he was perfectly capable of doing so.

One day Bill's teacher read out books made by some of the children to the whole class. Thus stimulated, Bill volunteered, 'I'll write about my clocks,' he said. 'Then you can read my book to anybody who wants to know how it's done.'

His teacher willingly made him an individual book. The results were disappointing. Bill filled the book with pictures and left it at that. 'The drawings are very good,' his teacher urged. 'But I don't know what you want me to say about them until you've written the words.'

Bill edged towards the investigation table. 'I don't want to write the words,' he complained. 'I want to make a sun-clock now.'

Had Bill been less capable, his teacher would have accepted the pictorial recording, but Bill knew he was well able to finish the job he had originally decided to do. 'I made you a special book,' his teacher persisted. 'I made it exactly as you wanted it. You must finish a page with words each day, because that's what you planned to do.' She kept a vigilant eye on Bill until his daily quota achieved the prescribed results. She then read the book to the class. 'It's a good book,' she rewarded his efforts. 'We can keep it in the reading corner.'

In each of these situations, the teacher was teaching the child how to work as an individual and without depending too extensively on adult assistance, or direction. She was also making him take the responsibility of fulfilling his obligations and of accepting the consequences of his own decision.

Some homes unwittingly fail to offer a child the right kind of choice, or an opportunity which fits his personal aptitudes. The unique qualities of a child certainly become evident in the protection of the family circle; even so, many aspects of personality may lie dormant, or little noticed, in the home. It takes the challenge of the wider world to spark off these hidden facets of personality. The teacher herself, as a significant and challenging adult, is basically responsible for detecting and nurturing personal qualities which even the most helpful home may not stir.

'I had no idea,' one parent said, 'that our Jenny was interested in things like music and dancing, and here she is, quite good at it. I don't know where she gets it from. Both her father and I and the two boys are more interested in books and in making things work, and she's never shown much interest in the things we do at home. I was beginning to think she's dull.' Jenny later gained a scholarship to a school of music and still remains the only musician in a family of highly successful individuals. Had it not been for a perceptive teacher, she might now be the least successful of the family.

In encouraging a child to make decisions, what are we asking him to do? To weigh up the pros and cons, to think logically and, having outlined the argument for and against, to make an objective judgement? At this stage in the child's development, it is scarcely that. Children can think at every stage but not in the way adults do, and many of the child's early decisions are based almost entirely on what he feels.

At this stage, it is the act of deciding, of going one's own way as opposed to following the way decided by someone else, that matters. Experience and maturity will enable the individual to back up his decisions with reasoning. In other words, choice and accepting its consequences, is a first step towards knowing the impregnable inner self which holds power over the individual and which no other can really penetrate.

This drive to assert his own independence is very strong in the child. It can bring him, of course, into conflict with authority and may involve him in a clash between gaining approval of those in authority and going his chosen way.

Gradually, decisions arising purely from feeling give way to elementary reasoning, in which the viewpoint of another can be assessed alongside one's own. 'I'm making a garage and I've got lots of cars so I want all the bricks.' John eyed Roy who was building a tower. For a moment he seemed about to claim what he wanted. John was strong for his age and victory was assured. Then he hesitated. 'But Roy started first, so I'll have to wait till he's done.' John had learned to compromise and later knew the satisfaction of deferring the gratification of egocentric desires until such time as this could be achieved without damage to another.

Sometimes adults can help, not by imposing moral attitudes on children, but by sharing the child's inner experience at its own level.

'You can't have all the bricks. That's selfish when someone

else wants to play with them too,' would have little effect on John in a moment of passionate desire. Whereas, 'Can't you start with the floor and I'll help you to lay out a plan. Then, when Roy's finished his tower, you could build up the walls,' might offer John the lead his reasoning power needs.

We cannot tell children what or how to think. We can try to share our thoughts and our thinking processes with them, and although they may appear to go along with us and agree or disagree at the appropriate moment, this doesn't mean they have assimilated thinking skills. What a child most needs is an adult whose mind stirs his own to action; who follows his elementary efforts to reason with understanding; who encourages him to formulate his own ideas and provide his own reasons; and then helps him to stand firm once the decision has been made.

The ultimate desire of the adult responsible for the child's upbringing and education, is for him to become a person, not with her mind, but with a mind of his own.

12

Imagination

Recent developments in education have led to many varied practices offering scope for imaginative experiences. Traditional patterns of education were designed round set and restricted standards of attainment. The divergent thinker didn't fit into the pattern. There was no means of measuring his merit. Imagination was unpredictable and therefore a threat to the establishment. The imaginative child had to learn to conform, otherwise he was frowned upon in school and often became a drop-out in the system.

Traditional methods guaranteed sound results, but in setting the sights of teachers and children on certain fixed goals, they restricted, and ultimately stifled, initiative and creative thinking, not only on the part of children, but in teachers as well. While some teachers accepted the security of the traditional programme others, with an unquenchable spirit of adventure, followed more imaginative paths. Many of these teachers recognised and valued the creative ability of children, and in their efforts to secure opportunities for children to develop these qualities, they shaped a new pattern in teaching and learning. It is to these imaginative teachers that we owe the liberal educational patterns which are shaping in Primary Schools today.

Imagination is the creative faculty of the mind. From his

earliest days the child stores experience in the form of images. These images are what is retained of visual, auditory, tactile and kinaesthetic impressions. Gradually the child develops the ability to summon these images, and to form and re-form mental patterns from his store of images. This faculty enables the child to recall impressions of past experiences which fit into current events; by comparing retained images with newly found impressions he uses previous experience to elucidate and expand the immediate. Imagination is that faculty which enables the child to use, as well as recall, images. By selecting and rearranging his images, the child can create a unique pattern, forecast a future event, or perceive the solution to a problem. An active imagination leads to creative learning, to learning which is full of meaning because it is linked with personal experience and therefore makes sense to the child.

The ability to think at any depth depends on the individual's powers of reflection, that is, on the ability of the mind to become conscious of its own operations. Reasoning involves the deliberate recall of past experience, the perception of its bearing on the immediate situation, the use of past experience to forecast the outcome of the immediate situation and to solve, in advance, problems which are likely to occur.

The images of the young child are acquired through sensory experiences of many kinds. Each sensory experience is embodied in how the child reacts emotionally at the moment it occurred. His images are a fusion of sensory and emotional impressions. This fusion of mind and feeling creates a need to express experience. A state of tension exists in the child which lends him insight together with a great thrust towards producing some outward evidence of his inner state. The way in which this inner experience is given outward expression depends on what the teacher provides. Even though verbal competence is an ultimate goal in education, to restrict the young child to words as his medium is to limit and even prohibit his creative impulses. In his early days, his vocabulary and modes of using it are limited. He needs many alternative modes of communication and experience in all of them, if he is to use the fruits of his stirring thoughts.

Imagination is not to be confused with simply that which is imagined. To ask the child to tell, or write, an imaginary story may offer little scope for imagination and is unlikely to provide a suitable channel of communication. How often did we as children, chew our pencils in a hopeless vacuum when asked to write the 'Day in the life of a Policeman' type of story. What we needed was the teeming richness of fresh colour, the cool damp plasticity of clay, the enchantment of musical sound, the temptation of space in which to move, the stimulation of simple props or a length of silk in a dressing-up box; then was the casement opened and we were free to wing away into a universe of our own creation. Some of us were fortunate enough to find such outlets at home. Those who didn't may still know little of that inner world of reality created by imagination.

As individuals we react to experience in very different ways, and the impressions and images we retain take on many different forms. Some people depend more on visual than on auditory images. Others make extensive use of tactile images and some find kinaesthetic memories more vivid and enduring.

In Primary Schools today, visual aids of all kinds are considered essential. Films, photographs, pictures and diagrams accompany unfamiliar material in teaching. Whenever possible the visual aid takes the form of a real object which can be handled as well as seen. A picture may serve to remind a child of what he has touched and physically seen, but it is always a poor substitute, and personal contact with reality is what leaves the most vivid impressions.

As the child grows older, he is expected to respond more often to pictorial substitutes for real objects. Teachers, in fact, depend very much on visual imagery, and it may be because this is the way many of them think. The children they teach may differ in this respect. Some children may respond more readily to auditory experiences and use auditory images in recall. Others may be more able to retain experiences which affect their muscles. Bodily movement, as we have seen in Chapter 5, has much to do with thinking, and what the child has physically experienced may be retained as kinaesthetic images. It is by no means a foregone conclusion that visual aids are the most helpful to all children.

A group of six- and seven-year-old children were taken to visit a fire station. The firemen were most co-operative. Not only did they talk to the children and show them the equipment, the children were allowed to handle the hose, to try on the helmets and to climb on to the engine and explore its various parts.

The children returned to school bursting with excitement. Their teacher hoped the visit would produce some imaginative writing and had prepared books of various sizes in which the children could draw, paint and write. But the children had ideas of their own. Dramatic play followed various themes suggested by their own movement experiences during the visit. One group of children created a 'fire' dance, and this gave rise to 'fire' music played on the chime bars. Another group turned to waste materials with ambitious plans for making a fire engine from boxes, tins and baking foil. A few children used paint as a means of expression, but not a single child showed any interest in writing.

At first as the children worked, they had little to say about the experience itself. They made various noises to represent the bell, water hissing from the hose, and the crackling flames. When they did use words it was more often in the form of questions than as a means of description. 'They need lots of water to put out a fire. Where does it all come from?' 'What happens if a little boy gets stuck at the top of some flats?' 'Are all the helmets the same size?' 'How long is the hose?'

Their teacher withheld any demands on these children for

written work. She gave them generous supplies of the materials they asked for, and answered their questions as well as she could.

Some weeks later, a fire in the neighbourhood revived the fire interest and the teacher was surprised by the accuracy of the children's impressions. This was when they started to talk about their fire experiences, and listening to them, the teacher realised the value of letting them use their own modes of communication earlier. It wasn't until the following term that some of the children turned to writing as a means of recalling and extending their fire experiences, and the quality of writing was obviously enhanced by their previous expressive work.

Sometimes a musical image is more vivid than a visual one. The atmosphere of foreign places, for instance, is more easily conveyed by music than by photographs. We catch the mood of a way of life which is foreign to our own. The music of a fandango, of a morris dance, or of an African tribal dance evokes bodily responses and is retained as an aural and bodily memory.

Perhaps we should look more carefully at the cult of visual aids and include at least a balance of auditory, tactile and kin-aesthetic aids. Visual education is not the most vital source of mental energy to every child. The trouble is, there is little to show when the sound is silenced, or the movement is stilled, and some teachers have learned to assess education by what they see as a result of it.

Like many other aspects of the child's development, imagination is active in the early years, and unless it is nurtured it can too easily fade or become stunted. It may become twisted with unfortunate results. While imagination is one of man's greatest gifts, distorted in growth, it can turn him into a delinquent or a neurotic.

Imaginative action on the part of the child leads to his first discoveries. What he discovers may be so familiar to adults as to have lost all interest, but to the child, experiencing for the first time, it is new and full of wonder, the reward of his own active imagination.

Anne was allowed to help mother with the washing up. She filled the dishpan to the brim and then began to put in the dishes. As she slipped the first cereal bowl into the brimming pan the water overflowed. Anne added another cereal bowl and again the water flowed over the brim of the pan. She squealed with pleasure, and added dish after dish, squealing each time the dishpan overflowed. It happened each time and she had discovered an interesting fact, because her mother understood the importance of her experience and let her delay the household chore until she had confirmed her discovery.

The adult who understands is willing to share the child's wonder and delight, to treat his discoveries with all the respect due to the one who makes them. He is not discouraged by being told, 'Anybody knows that. There's nothing new in that.' In this way the child's imagination is nourished and encouraged to develop so that he retains and uses his imaginative powers instead of losing them.

The truly sensitive adult does more than nurture, he also stimulates. Stimulation takes many forms. The teacher can either stir the child directly through personal experience, or indirectly by relating him to the imaginative experiences of others.

Stimulation through direct personal experience is associated with objects and situations which are aesthetically pleasing. It is also associated with the challenge of problematic situations. Natural phenomena, well-designed pottery, objects of great beauty, fascinating rock formations, sand under a microscope; the range of materials with which teachers can confront the child are infinite in their variety. Each will stir a child in a unique way, providing the child is allowed to make his uninterrupted face-to-face relationship with them.

The inspiration of such contact may be experienced by the child first as an inward reality. Usually the child seeks some means of externalising such experience, and if appropriate materials are available, he will turn to these. In clay or paint, fabric or musical sound, words or movement, the child may recreate his inward experience and so come face to face with it. He will extend and deepen the experience for his own benefit, communicating with himself. He may also share the experience with others, communicating with those who take an interest in what he has created.

The challenge of problematic situations may make even greater demands on the child's imagination. The teacher may be asked by the child, for example, to provide a 'piece of velvet to make a dolly's dress'. The teacher can either produce a piece of a suitable size, and help the child to cut out the correct shape, or she can offer the child several pieces with the restriction, 'You may have one of these pieces. Find out from which one the dress can be cut without wasting any material. Then I will let you use it.' In this situation the child experiences a certain amount of tension. She can't find out by trial and error. She must use her judgement. She may manœuvre the pattern pieces around, but she may not cut. Her imaginative qualities are brought to the fore and will help her to perceive the solution.

In the following situation, Andy, a rather unimaginative six-year-old, was presented with a problem by his mother when he needed a new battery for his toy car. 'I bought a spare for you,' she told him, 'but it's on the top shelf and I can't reach it because the plumber's left his tool-kit in front of the shelves. You'll have to wait until he's gone.'

She went upstairs and Andy, who very much wanted to carry on with his game, eyed the shelves and the bulky kit in front of them. He couldn't stand on that, and, even if he could, he wouldn't be able to reach the top shelf. He fetched a kitchen stool and stood on top of it. The desired battery was still out of reach. He fetched a second stool, but even balanced on top of the first it didn't improve the situation.

The two stools stood, one on each side of the tool kit, and something familiar in their physical relationship stirred Andy's imagination. He fetched the ironing board, and, using it as a plank, he made a bridge between the stools. In great excitement he tested the bridge. It cleared the tool kit, and by standing on it, he was just able to reach the desired battery.

Andy's sense of achievement was greater than his sense of satisfaction in being able to carry on with his game. His ingenuity surprised his mother to such an extent that she forgot to reprimand him. 'Andy's got something about him after all,' she told his father later in the day.

The imaginative experience of others can spark imagination in even the duller child. Poetry and literature, painting, sculpture, inventions and scientific discovery, only the best work of the masters is good enough for children. They may not understand the poetry of Wordsworth in an intellectual sense, but they can appreciate its ring of truth and the author's skilful use of words.

The child and the artist in any field have much in common; each is struggling to create, in tangible form, ideas and impressions which stir the mind and demand expression. The child, fresh from his own struggles with materials such as clay, paint, wood, notes, movement, words, which lend themselves to the artist yet challenge and frustrate because they are not easy to handle, is highly sensitive to what the masters have to say.

The works of Van Gogh, Gauguin and Turner have particular appeal. A teacher of four- and five-year-old children had a box full of prints mounted on stout card. Many of the children enjoyed taking out the cards one at a time and chattering to one another about them. They made up stories about the subjects in the paintings. They told one another why they liked a particular picture, and sometimes why they didn't like one. Sometimes it was the use of colour that impressed them, but they also noticed the artist's sympathetic treatment. 'I love that chair,' said one little girl. 'It looks so bundly and I'd like to sit on it.' The love of these children for their pictures clearly affected the way they used paint themselves.

A teacher of seven- and eight-year-old children was interested in the lives of inventors. He told the children exciting stories about the development of television, of moving pictures, of electricity and of other inventions with which the children were already familiar. He called his stories, 'In the footsteps of . . .' and the children acknowledged his aptitude as an author by asking him to 'Tell us about how matches came,' or 'Who first thought about wheels?', or 'How did clocks start?'

Sometimes the teacher was able to use facts from the lives of real people. At other times he used such facts as were available and created imaginary characters to people, for instance, the plains of Mesopotamia where man was struggling to transport goods and very much needed the wheel.

In this teacher's room the investigation table was of paramount importance to the children. They felt able to identify with the ingenious originators of bygone days. One group of boys assembled the parts of many discarded clocks and watches. They made tiny replicas of windmills, cranes, water-wheels and other working models. One ambitious model included a replica of the Nile 'in Bible times' complete with an irrigation system operated by an 'Archimedes Screw'. When they learned that these screws are still in use, they were filled with respect for a way of life which had persisted through thousands of years.

In situations such as these, each child is encouraged to think and imagine in his own unique way. His mind is being fed with what stimulates thought, rather than with facts and information which are easily measured by tests. Examination restrictions leave little room for the divergent thinker, and it is often the child who obeys the rules who scores higher than the imaginative child whose thoughts run on more creative lines. If we do not find a place for the inventor, the unorthodox thinker, the investigator of a fresh line of enquiry, or the contemplative as opposed to the traditional doer, then the educational system will perpetuate only what already exists and society will stand still.

And who is to know which of our children will become the leader of tomorrow's generation? The workings of imagination are not always easy to recognise, and as teachers we have a great responsibility for the survival of imagination. It can so easily get lost in childhood, and once imagination has been allowed to die, it is very difficult to restore.

Imagination is often an awkward quality to deal with in other people, but without it man will become little more than any other in the animal kingdom. In the race towards good jobs and the competitive effort directed towards successful mediocrity, imagination can be submerged or die of neglect. It is often up to the teacher to rescue the child from the good intentions of ambitious parents, and teachers must not fail in this responsibility. In order to succeed, teachers need the support of those who employ them. New ways of teaching and learning will only develop successfully where they are unhampered by too many limited academic demands. We must leave teachers free to teach in an imaginative way if children are to become imaginative adults.

13

The child as an artist

In this age of the supermarket, concern for increased production and higher living standards dominates human endeavour. Education is seen as a means of preparing each citizen for his contribution to the national economy; non-productive pursuits fall into disrepute. The bank manager, the lawyer and the doctor are high-ranking professionals, while the artist, the contemplative and the creative thinker are left to struggle unaided. The impoverished artist and the inventor whose patent right expires for lack of funds are common amongst us.

Present-day values leave many of us feeling uneasy, wondering where the educational system fits into the picture. Universal education has been established as the right of every citizen, and in our particular culture, at least ten years of a person's life is devoted to making him educated.

Much of what we are taught we forget, but what we are as people remains, and the ultimate effect of education is enshrined in adult personality. What a person has made of himself is what education is about, and what motivates the adult is the outcome of attitudes he has acquired during the course of being educated. Those of us who are responsible for education must surely acknowledge that if adult attitudes are in question, the fault lies in education itself, not in those who receive education.

To get to the core of the problem we must study both the

beginning and the end of the learning process. What is there in the nature of the child as he embarks on learning which suggests his ultimate destiny, and what is it in the last analysis that man aspires to?

Observation of the young child leads us to suppose that he is essentially creative and imaginative, and at heart an artist and a thinker. His exploratory approach to his environment enables him first of all to discover the characteristics and behaviour of primitive materials, and then to use them according to purposes devised by his imagination. He has a natural urge to make his mark, and delights in sympathetic and responsive materials such as mud and clay, sand and wood, which retain for him his own unique impressions. Given the right opportunity, an intimate relationship grows up between the child and his materials, and what is created is the outcome of this relationship, some unique product which depends on what has happened between them.

Through his creative use of materials, the child is brought face to face with himself. The intimately responsive clay retains his impressions, revealing to him aspects of his own nature. The feelings and images he retains as a result of experience are reproduced in visible form. In his marks, on whatever surface, the unique imprint of a person is held.

The child also uses materials as a means of clarifying and extending experience. Imagination may be fired by his first glimpse of a liner gliding out to sea. He tries, with the materials available, to reproduce the impression, to find out more about the shape of the liner and to speculate on what makes it move. He isn't satisfied with the knowledge acquired through the evidence of his senses, he seeks to extend it and turns to the adult for help. His finished model is visible evidence of his deep interest and the very shape of it echoes his own personality. The whole creation is characteristic of him.

Through working with his materials, the child is made aware of his strengths and weaknesses. Faced with a problem, does he persist, or is he easily defeated? Does he enjoy the challenge of experimenting with adhesives until he finds the one which does the job effectively? Can he plan and organise? Does he tend to lead because he has good ideas and can visualise ahead of construction? Or does he prefer to execute with care and precision the ideas promoted by others? Does he work at his materials impelled by an idea or feeling which won't let him rest until it has been given shape and form? Or does he use materials as a means of reproducing what he has seen others make? Through his work with materials the child gets to know himself.

Unless he is taught to the contrary, the growing child applies his artistic principles to many types of materials, and he can become as much an artist in his use of words or mathematical ideas as he is with paint, or paper and paste.

What is more, young children are extremely sensitive to their materials, and a profound need to explore their feelings and their intellectual reactions to the world of experiences finds its outlet in the use they make of everything they can manipulate.

At the adult end of the story is Man's search for immortality. So full is man of wonder at himself he finds it difficult to believe that he can ever cease to be, and his sense of self-fulfilment finds expression in the ideas he has about his divine and incorruptible nature. Is it man the economist, or man the artist which survives?

A visitor in Crete stands amongst the ruins of a magnificent civilisation. What remains of the fabulous Minoan Empire stirs his imagination. It is easy to envisage those people in 1500 or even 3000 BC as he examines the mosaics, the well-designed pottery, the amazing architecture and the efficient plumbing system. In these remains an ancient people present their message to many generations. It is the artist amongst them who found a means of projecting the image of a magnificent civilisation into the future. The creative and imaginative factors in man are what gives him a claim to divinity, and man the artist is his own means of immortality.

Man's work as an artist is not restricted to music, art and craftsmanship. The 'useful' subjects such as English and mathematics are equally the field of the artist. When we follow the child in his natural modes of learning, we help him to understand his mother tongue through the way in which he personally uses it, to understand mathematical ideas through discovering his own mathematics and creating his own modes of using numbers.

All that the child learns should have personal relevance and be understood by him as contributory to the great creative business of being alive. Getting a good job means finding a role in the community which brings, not only self-fulfilment, but a sense of being essential in the community. It isn't examination results which secure such a job. Fundamentally it is what the adult is as a person which makes the job and equips him to achieve self-fulfilment, and nowhere is the child more of an artist than in the shaping of himself.

There are amongst us today, some who regard themselves as 'anti-progressive'. 'Let's stop thinking of the child as a creator or an explorer,' they say, 'who is allowed to go his own way in a do-as-you-like environment, and get him down to some good hard work. He is immature and is incapable of producing thoughts of his own, or of shaping his own destiny. We as adults know better than he and we must tell him what to think and be, if he is to become a useful person.' With the best of intentions, these 'anti-progressives' feel it their duty to perpetuate the kind of society they live in and to turn out future citizens cast in their own mould.

There are those who sneer at the idea of children discovering what has already been discovered by preceding generations. 'It is unrealistic to speak of discovery methods,' they complain, 'unless the child is to reveal something not previously known, and that's impossible.' They seem to forget those moments when, as children, they first realised that sugar vanishes completely in hot tea, or that a mixture of yellow and blue produces green, or that $3+5+1$ gives the same result as $1+5+3$. In such illuminating moments they were in truth discoverers.

The way we attempt to bring up the child depends on the view we hold of him. Is each child an embryonic person capable, with the help of experienced adults, of designing his own life style, of taking a hand in the creation of his own personality? Or do we see the child as pliable material from which we mould a suitable citizen, carefully designed by adults to perpetuate existing society?

Clinical studies of the young child all point to his unique nature and force us to acknowledge his aptitude for becoming a person with a mind of his own making. It is arrogant to suppose that we can do the job for him.

But the child cannot create from nothing, and the essential role of the adult is to provide, first of all the right kind of materials, and then an environment in which the growth of his relationship with these materials can take place.

Essential among the materials from which his mind and personality are fashioned is something to think about. We can share our thoughts with the child. We can provide access for him to the thoughts of others. We can turn his attention to what is worth thinking about, but we cannot do his thinking for him. We can show the child what he might understand, but we cannot show him how to understand it; we are forced to leave him alone in doing that.

Most important of all, we can welcome the child's own thoughts when he is prepared to share them with us, and we can share his exploratory adventures in thinking as often as we expect him to share ours. We may share his thoughts and we may tell him about our thoughts, but we cannot give our thoughts to him. Nor should we try, for our thoughts are born of today, while his thoughts will come to fruition tomorrow.

In this book we have considered the growth of thinking in

the young child and we have now reached a point where we should try to identify the basic features of this growth pattern and outline the way in which the child structures his mind. It is the artist again in the child which is responsible for the creation of his patterns of thought.

The starting point is in the child's movements. From his inborn ability to grasp and to move from point to point, he gradually constructs a magnificent range of motor activities, from dancing and standing still to speaking and writing.

As a result of these movements the child enables his senses to obtain messages from his environment. His senses make use of the impressions received in two ways. As a result of perception, the effect of what the child sees, hears and touches is retained as images, and these images can be visual, aural, tactile or kinaesthetic As a result of sensation the child retains emotional impressions, or feelings, about the contacts he makes through his senses. He now has memory material in the form of images and feelings with which to recreate, or create, in mental form the experiences he has had, those he would like to have, and those he may have at some later date. Images and feelings are the material of the mind, and from them the child creates his thoughts. Without them he would have no thoughts, and if the quality of his impressions is poor, then his thoughts are likewise impoverished.

The material of thought can be impoverished or enriched depending on two factors: the effectiveness of the child's sense organs and the quality of the environment in which they operate. Adults are responsible for ensuring that the child's sight, hearing and sense of touch are as healthy as possible, or that the child is provided with aids to improve them. Adults are also responsible for the range of quality of the child's environment. These things they may attend to, but no matter how hard they try, they cannot make the thoughts that emerge from the child's mind.

Adults may believe that they have put a thought into a

child's mind. What happens is that the child is given information about a thought which exists in the adult's mind. The information can be verbal, pictorial or musical and the child may endeavour to reproduce it in similar form, but unless he has used his creative powers and made the thought his own, his information merely echoes what he received, and thinking at any depth has not taken place. He may even develop the habit of retaining information and retelling it on request, but there is little connection between this and the assimilation and accommodation of experience which is a prerequisite of thought.

If we acknowledge from the start that the child approaches thought activity in much the same way as he approaches other of his creative materials, then we can begin to understand what is going on in his mind, because we are no longer preoccupied with the futile task of trying to fashion his mind for him.

In this privileged position we can observe the slow evolutionary growth of thought and personality in the young child as he endeavours to become what is in him to be. Thus we may help him to create and give himself to the society in which he is reared.

This is our job, and if we are not prepared to take such a humble view of it, then it were better that we turned our attention elsewhere. For in the creation of himself the child knows better than anyone else what he can become and where he is to go.

The child starts off as an artist with a mind of his own. He is equipped to become the architect of his own personality and ultimate destiny. Each child by nature sets off in the right direction. If as an adult he doesn't arrive, we should ask those responsible for his education, what has happened? Is this the best we can do? What steps can be taken to secure for man his rightful heritage?

Appendix

Although our knowledge of children's thinking is still in its infancy, much has been written about it. We could compile a lengthy and highly erudite bibliography which might impress the student yet remain unread by the practising teacher.

Teachers are busy people. They have a full-time job to do in developing workable theory from their own observation and practices. When they read they want to get to the core of the matter as quickly as possible.

For this reason I have provided a very small selection of books based on personal choice. A brief outline of the contents of each will, I hope, enable any teacher to select a book which best fits her interest and teaching situation.

These books, all recently published, have impressed and interested me, and I think they will be of equal interest to other practitioners.

A Child's Mind
MURIEL BEADLE
MacGibbon and Kee (UK), Doubleday, paper (US), 1971

Muriel Beadle believes in the power of the general public to shape the educational system, and she sets out in this book to disseminate information about cognitive growth amongst lay-people. She reviews recently published research on the mental development of children, paying particular attention to learning in the earliest years of life.

Mrs Beadle communicates in lucid terms. She has a lively and highly readable style. From a vast accumulation of information she selects what is relevant and fascinating, and interesting biographical notes help to bring to life many great research workers who have contributed to our understanding of the growth of the child's mind.

Mrs Beadle emphasises the inter-relation between heredity and environment. 'Human babies', she says, 'are not passive receivers of experience . . . the younger the child, the greater the effect of environment upon his genetic potential.'

She defines intelligence as 'a mode of behaviour', something which children grow. The potential for this growth is in the genes, but its quality is determined by environmental factors. The emotional environment surrounding the child is of signal importance in cognitive development.

The book is written against an American background and the shadow of racial problems haunts the chapters on cultural and social influences. Nevertheless, her message is clear to all who are interested in children and their education. Promoters of pre-school education, in particular, will find much in her book to provoke thought and support action.

This is an impressive study which deals with the how and the why of learning rather than with methods of training or teaching. For teachers who want facts and information without searching through a library, this is the place to find it.

The Thinking Class
EDWARD DE BONO
Ward Lock Educational, 1970

'There is a huge unrecognised interest in the subject of thinking,' says Edward de Bono. Wherever he is billed to lecture on the subject he has a capacity audience. He gives essentially the same lecture to senior executives at the London Graduate School of Business as he does to Goldsmiths' College and he finds that hippies, artists, research scientists and business executives exhibit a universal interest in the basic nature of thinking, the neglect of the subject in the school curriculum and its fundamental importance in the modern world.

'I wonder', he speculates, 'if we shall look back one day and find it difficult to believe that there was a time when thinking was not an established part of the school curriculum.' He questions the assumption that thinking is effectively taught as a by-product of other subjects and outlines the case for treating it directly as a specialist subject. Few people are satisfied, he feels, with the amount of thinking skill developed by education. The sheer increase in present-day knowledge makes it more necessary than ever before to establish thinking as a subject in its own right.

The use a person makes of intelligence depends on his skill in thinking, and thinking strategies can be learned and used in a similar manner to mathematical techniques. Like other skills, the basic principles of thinking can be taught from the age of five.

He sees thinking as a universal subject which can be taught by anyone, and he suggests that every parent or teacher should spend an hour a week with a child on the subject. Thinking as a subject should be free from examination, which would kill it by making it too formal and self-conscious.

The contents of this pamphlet could be assimilated in half an hour.

Piaget For Teachers
HANS G. FURTH
Prentice-Hall, 1970

Professor Furth has first-hand knowledge of Piaget, with whom he worked for a year. He addresses himself to teachers in a series of charming letters, and outlines the educational revolution which an enlightened acceptance of Piaget's theory could bring to our schools. Although his argument is directed towards American teachers who are working in the strait-jacket of a fixed curriculum, there is much in his notion of a 'school of thinking' which demands the attention of teachers and parents everywhere.

In Hans Furth's opinion, Piaget's findings point to the need to 'strengthen his (the child's) thinking so that the child will develop to the point where he can use the verbal medium intelligently'. He is convinced that we concentrate too much on imparting specialised skills, such as reading. Thinking, he says, comes before language, and adults have little idea of the quality of thinking that goes on in the child, because they exaggerate the role of language in the development of thinking.

Furth believes that the ability to think and to learn can be cultivated, and he describes a number of thinking games based on symbol-picture logic which are designed to challenge the child's operative intelligence and reinforce his spontaneous thinking development.

Readers may find some difficulty in comprehending Furth's interpretation of Piaget's theory of intelligence as a basis on which to construct the educational treatment of the child. They may question the ultimate purpose of his thinking exercises and be severely shaken by criticism of their faith in early literacy. But they will find a study of his letters an intellectually invigorating experience which leaves them with plenty to think about.

What We Owe Children: The Subordination of Teaching to Learning
CALEB GATTEGNO
Routledge & Kegan Paul (UK), Avon, paper (US), 1971

Gattegno maintains that with the intelligent use of the powers of the mind in all individuals a radical transformation would occur in the classroom.

Much current teaching, he argues, exploits the faculty of memory which is the weakest of the mental powers available for intelligent use. The alternative to the use of memory is to build up the strengths of children, which he calls the functionings of children, and use these as the basis of education. The child learns to sit, to eat, and to speak successfully through his own mental powers, and the teacher should construct what he learns in school on what he has accomplished before he enters.

Education should provide a means of changing time into experience, instead of merely filling up time, as it often does at present, with those devices such as exercises, homework, reviewing and testing which are designed only to transmit knowledge.

This is a scholarly and fascinating exposition of some fundamental issues in learning and teaching. Teachers who are familiar with *Words in Colour*, his approach to reading which uses colour as a signalling system, may feel that his own practice doesn't illuminate his principles.

All the same, this book merits serious study and should help to clarify some of the aims and objectives of present-day education.

Nursery Schools for All
JILL and PENDARELL KENT
Ward Lock Educational (UK), International Publications Service (US), 1970

As a work of reference in the field of pre-school education, this book is unique. It is packed with facts and information, and offers detailed guidance on all matters affecting the education of the under-fives.

The authors write from personal experience. They put a strong case for nursery education and examine its theoretical justification against the background of the current debate on progressive methods of teaching. They are not afraid to express firm views on controversial issues.

Few teachers have the time to study the various and often conflicting findings of research workers in any depth, and they will appreciate the skill with which relevant information is selected and presented to provide a summary of essential work in early development.

While experienced teachers may not agree with some of the educational ideas expressed, they will acknowledge the thoroughly practical way in which theory is interpreted in the organisation of active learning.

The Growth of Understanding in Mathematics
KENNETH LOVELL
Holt, Rinehart and Winston, Inc., 1971

Kenneth Lovell has the gift of being able to make a simple analysis of very difficult ideas. Our knowledge of the growth of thinking in children is still in its infancy but Piaget's work provides us with a means of comprehending the growth of children's understanding. The trouble is Piaget is difficult to study and we must often depend on the interpretation of his ideas by others. We can turn with confidence to Dr Lovell's work for this service.

This book deals essentially with children's understanding of mathematical concepts. Lovell is concerned with the relationship between 'the quality of thinking skills of the child and the complexity of the mathematical ideas to which he is introduced'. In simple lucid terms he outlines the growth of the child's mental structures and describes the characteristics of each stage in mental growth. He uses the child's reactions to mathematical experiences to illustrate his points and summarises the major factors affecting the growth of thinking.

He also examines the role of language in this process. 'Language', he says, 'helps the child to organise his experience and carry his thoughts with precision, and this can only be brought about by dialogue and discussion alongside action.'

Always, he maintains, intuitive understanding on the part of the teacher must complement what we know of learning in scientific terms.

The major part of this book is devoted to a study of the mathematical ideas a teacher should introduce to children, with suggestions as to the kinds of activities which might help a child to understand and use these ideas. The core of this book, however, has far-reaching implications, and it offers enlightenment to the teacher who studies it.

On Children's Thinking

PROFESSOR E. A. LUNZER
Printed for the University of Nottingham by Hawthornes of Nottingham

The inaugural lecture delivered by Professor Lunzer in the Portland Lecture Hall, University of Nottingham on 13th November 1969

Lunzer's 'main concern is not to detail the views of a particular individual, even a pioneer (Piaget), but rather to sketch in the outline of the present state of knowledge, and to suggest what look like significant gaps'.

He suggests four distinct phases in the development of children's thinking, using examples from his own observation to illustrate the factors which characterise each stage. While his characterisation follows closely on that of Piaget, it is simpler and based on psychological rather than logical reasoning. He also indicates questions which can only be answered on the basis of further research. He suggests, for example, that we need to examine the assumption that discovery methods are somehow justified by the work of Piaget. We need to resolve the very active debate on the precise role of language in conceptual development.

'In the end we want to know what the child is doing when he is learning and what the teacher is doing when he is teaching.'

And this, he declares, is his intention during the years ahead.

Readings in Educational Psychology: Learning and Teaching
E. STONES
Methuen and Co. (UK), Barnes and Noble (US), 1970

This book provides a sound and readable starting point for those students and teachers who seek to improve their work in the classroom through a study of what the educational psychologist has to tell us.

Authoritative statements from leading workers in a number of fields have been selected and edited by Stones in the hope that they will throw some light on the nature and conditions of classroom learning with particular emphasis on cognitive aspects.

While attention is paid to the significance of pre-language experience in the formation of concepts, the crucial influence of language in the development of mental processes is carefully examined. The teacher is seen as a key element in the learning situation, and careful consideration is given to her function in optimising the child's learning.

An attempt is made to define the exact nature of discovery learning and to clarify the different, but complementary contributions made by discovery and rote learning in the total educational enterprise.

The teacher who studies research is usually overwhelmed by the sheer volume of conflicting evidence and there is still a serious gap between researchers and the teacher in the classroom. Stones does much to bridge this gap and offer guidance about the relationship between findings from research into learning and educational practice.

This is a book to study rather than read, and teachers could very well start with the excellent simplicity of J. B. Carroll's papers on *Words, Meanings and Concepts*.

Six Psychological Studies
JEAN PIAGET *Translation edited by* DAVID ELKIND
University of London Press (UK), Random House, paper
(US), 1968

These six essays form a summary and a helpful introduction
to Piaget's work. They deal with the stages in mental development of the child, the relation between thought and language
and the interaction between nature and nurture. In an
introduction to the work, Dr Elkind describes Piaget's major
themes and comments on the value of his work.

Dr Elkind makes the important point that Piaget nowhere
points to the practical implications of his work. Some educators
engage in certain teaching practices in the name of Piaget. In
such cases it is the educator's interpretation of Piaget which is
being utilised and not Piaget's own ideas about educational
practice. It is doubtful indeed whether we have yet established
a solid foundation of theory from which practical implications
can be drawn.

These essays place Piaget's contribution in proper perspec-
tive. While they make no attempt to suggest what should be
taught or how the teacher should help the child, they will
deepen the understanding of teachers and enable them to
interpret the behaviour of young children with greater
accuracy.

This is a book for the serious student who is searching for
personal enlightenment rather than for guidance in pedagogical
performance.

The Critical Years: Early Childhood Education at the Crossroads
EMMY LOUISE WIDMER
International Textbook Company (UK), Intext Educational Publishers (US), 1970

The aim of this book is to encourage the development of understanding about young children which will lead to education designed round the individuality of each child. It forms a comprehensive survey of the what, the how and the why of education in early childhood, and expresses a strong plea for protecting children against the pressures to hasten learning and produce 'instant adults'.

Dr Widmer stresses the importance of sincere observation of the child and feels that understanding of him comes more from the intimate knowledge of the individual adult than from research proof.

The text includes a study of the role of concept formation in the child's learning and thinking, the part played by nutrition and the special problems of dealing with children who are physically and emotionally impoverished.

The exuberant American style of writing is perhaps off-putting to British teachers, yet they will find in it an informed and interesting study of the five-year-old and his educational opportunities.

A real attempt is made in this book to relate effective early childhood learning and teaching to modern theory. It also offers insight into the attitudes of those responsible for the education of young children in the United States.

Index

Topics which are clearly indicated by chapter headings are not included in this index.

Also by Alice Yardley

Young Children Learning

This series is designed to express, as clearly as possible, current educational theory in terms of the practical work of teachers and children in infant schools.

The four books in the series, *Reaching Out, Exploration and Language, Discovering the Physical World* and *Senses and Sensitivity*, incorporate the most recent research into the ways in which children develop and learn. They are illuminated throughout by plenty of factual examples from classroom situations, and each book covers a range of topics connected with some particular aspect of the child's life in school. Not only teachers but parents and students in colleges of education will find these books a constant source of inspiration and guidance.

Reaching Out

Capturing the joy shared by adults and children who are privileged to live and work in the infant schools of today, *Reaching Out* provides the foundation on which the other books in the series are based although each book is complete in itself. It is about all our children—not about abstract nouns like 'intelligence'—and demonstrates clearly the truism that to want to learn is far, far more important than to be taught.

Exploration and Language

This is not a book about the teaching of reading or the development of speech or the acquisition of skill in original writing. It is a book about a gift peculiar to man, about his ability to abstract, to symbolise, to create a world of imagination from the material he garners through his experience of things and situations.

Exploring his world leads to the development of language, and in man's use of symbols his understanding of his world is clearly perceived. The early stages in the development of this understanding are examined and appraised in this book about the child and his words.

Discovering the Physical World

Exploration is the way a child lives, and the world today abounds in opportunities to investigate not only natural but technical phenomena in an environment where so much is made by man. The third book in the series is basically an examination of the way in which children begin to develop mathematical and scientific ideas. The aim of the teacher is to ensure sound development of these basic ideas, but none of the teachers whose work is quoted were either mathematicians or scientists. They were all women teachers, many of them married with children of their own, who made the effort to acquaint themselves more fully with their surroundings. Teachers whose powers of mathematical and scientific thought are undeveloped may feel encouraged by these records to adventure themselves into the child's wonderful world of discovery.

Senses and Sensitivity

If education is to be of service to the individual, it must offer him opportunities for growth in every aspect of his person. It must be concerned as much with the language of feeling as with knowledge and skills. A well-informed mind is of no use, either to its owner or to society, unless its contents can be liberated, and this education in communication should range over many diverse fields. In *Senses and Sensitivity* Alice Yardley expresses some of her own deepest beliefs about the nature of education and records many profound experiences which have enriched her own life.

The Teacher of Young Children

The demands made upon the teacher of young children are many, varied and increasing, and to be effective she needs to evaluate them, to plan her working and to establish her own order of priorities. This book helps the reader by examining the work of practising teachers and by suggesting practical solutions to some of the teaching problems.